D0307889

Governing Sustainable Cities

Bob Evans, Marko Joas,
Susan Sundback
and
Kate Theobald

EARTHSCAN

London • Sterling, VA

First published by Earthscan in the UK and USA in 2005

ISBN: 1-84407-169-3 paperback
       1-84407-168-5 hardback

Typesetting by JS Typesetting Ltd, Wellingborough, Northants
Printed and bound in the UK by Cromwell Press, Trowbridge
Cover design by Ruth Bateson

For a full list of publications please contact:

Earthscan
8–12 Camden High Street
London, NW1 0JH, UK
Tel: +44 (0)20 7387 8558
Fax: +44 (0)20 7387 8998
Email: earthinfo@earthscan.co.uk
Web: www.earthscan.co.uk

22883 Quicksilver Drive, Sterling, VA 20166-2012, USA

Earthscan is an imprint of James and James (Science Publishers) Ltd and publishes
in association with WWF-UK and the International Institute for Environment and
Development

A catalogue record for this book is available from the British Library

Library of Congress Cataloging-in-Publication Data
Governing sustainable cities / Bob Evans ... [et al.].
      p. cm.
   Includes bibliographical references and index.
   ISBN 1-84407-169-3 (pbk.) – ISBN 1-84407-168-5 (hardback)
  1. City planning–Environmental aspects–Europe. 2. Local government–Europe.
3. Sustainable development–Europe–Citizen participation. I. Evans, Bob, 1947 October
17-
   HT169.E85G68 2005
   307.1'216'094–dc22
                                                                    2004019518

Contents

List of Figures, Tables and Boxes

FIGURES

TABLES

BOXES

Preface

Urban local authorities have been some of the most committed institutions working towards sustainable development during the last decade. A survey undertaken by the International Council for Local Environmental Initiatives (ICLEI) in preparation for the World Summit on Sustainable Development (WSSD) in Johannesburg, South Africa, in 2002 showed that over 6000 local authorities had started Local Agenda 21 or similar planning processes, with their citizens, the aim being to develop strategies for future development that reconcile a good quality of life with the need to reduce the use of natural resources. In 2000, a consortium of European research partners coordinated by ICLEI began to investigate the outcomes of Local Agenda 21 processes in European cities and towns in the framework of a project entitled Local Authorities' Self-Assessment of Local Agenda (LASALA). The project (which analysed some 150 municipalities in a two-stage exercise) identified 24 cases of 'good practice' for sustainability. Although these cases originate from many different countries and thus represent different cultural, political and economic framework conditions, one question that remained unanswered was: are there any common factors and conditions that allow good practice to occur?

To date, there has been a widely accepted assumption amongst both re-searchers and practitioners that one way of spreading innovation in local policy is through documentation and dissemination of good examples, which are then transferred, adapted and further developed from one place to another. But what if this transfer fails? What if there are preconditions that have to be fulfilled before a local sustainability process can produce tangible results? To answer these questions, the same research partners formed a new consortium and started to look in greater depth at the processes operating within European cities and towns – in particular, considering those that had already been identified as implementing 'good practice' in local sustainability. The project in which this assessment was conducted is entitled Developing Institutional and Social Capacities for Urban Sustainability (DISCUS), and its results are presented in this book.

The DISCUS project contributes to the ongoing debate about the relationship between 'government' and 'governance'; but it has had a further aim: to analyse the links between these processes and sustainable development policy processes. Local governments from across Europe usually consider a participatory approach to governing a town or city as being an integral part of sustainable development. In fact, a majority of the 'good practice' cases are 'successful' in the way that the local authority works together with interest organizations and involves citizens in a dialogue about the future of their municipality. So, is this a contribution to sustainable development?

The common assumption here is that this shift from a top-down ('government') to a more dialogue-oriented ('governance') approach increases awareness, shared responsibility and acceptance among citizens of the necessary, yet so far unpopular, policy steps towards less resource use and better social inclusion. This suggests that at some stage in the future, citizens – encouraged by this shift and led by their local governments – take ownership of their municipality and respond in a spirit of cooperation to the challenge of sustainability. This may sound idealistic and, indeed, it requires a good deal of stepping back from immediate short-term interests for both local government and civil society. For this to happen, certain capacities have to be built up and in place before local 'government' and 'governance' will contribute to more 'sustainability'.

In order to examine and understand the forms of institutional and social capacities that are required for sustainable development policy achievements, the DISCUS fieldworkers undertook research in 40 cities and towns all over Europe. The analysis of the enormous amount of data gathered during the one year of fieldwork confirms that a shift from 'government' to 'governance' is not sufficient to create more sustainable towns and cities. While it is clear that the rules of interaction between local governments and civil society need to be modified in order to prevent the sustainability agenda from running against citizens, rather than taking them on board, strong and self-confident local governments are central in bringing about tangible and long-term results for sustainability.

The 'art' of *Governing Sustainable Cities* is thus to create competent local governments that, in interaction with a highly responsible (and responsive) civil society, apply a form of governing that brings about the most sustainable solutions. Building up the institutional and social capacity needed in order to achieve this goes beyond weekend courses in new public management or an 'environment day' every year. It is a long-term process that includes education and awareness-raising, but also the creation of a new societal attitude of shared responsibility for the public welfare (or the 'common goods'), which at present seems to be a straight contradiction to the current paradigm of individualism and enhanced competition.

However, if there is any 'entrance door' to building up this capacity for 'governing for sustainable development', then it is local government: a local government that has genuine concern – not only for the interests of its elected or professional representatives, but for the 'common good' of its municipality – while at the same time engaging in a continuous local debate with civil society of what the 'common good' of the city actually is. *Governing Sustainable Cities* is about changing local governments and thus local society in order to come to a form of local governing that fertilizes local sustainability. This may sound confusing and, in fact, requires more than just applying a handful of new methods of managing a town or city. However, I hope the DISCUS project and its results can help in clarifying these concepts and their interrelations; certainly, it will outline a number of those 'ingredients' needed to enable more sustainable towns and cities to emerge.

I would like to express my thanks to the DISCUS project consortium – composed of the Sustainable Cities Research Institute at Northumbria University,

Åbo Akademi University, FocusLab srl, Universidade Nova de Lisboa, WWF-UK, and the two consultation partners: the European Sustainable Cities and Towns Campaign and the Regional Environmental Centre – for three years of highly inspiring and often intensive, yet always enjoyable discussion and trustful cooperation. On behalf of this team, my thanks also extend to the group of fieldworkers without whom the data for this book would not exist; our academic Advisory Board and our Panel of Practitioners for their critical feedback and encouragement; and the European Commission's Directorate-General for Research Fifth Framework Programme, which largely co-funded the DISCUS project.

Stefan Kuhn
ICLEI – Local Governments for Sustainability, European Secretariat,
Freiburg, Germany
DISCUS coordinator
October 2004

Acknowledgements

This book has been written by the authors on behalf of the DISCUS project consortium, and we wish to fully acknowledge the role that the consortium partners have played in planning and undertaking the research upon which this book is based. We also thank them for their valuable contribution to the analysis, which is presented here. Although we emphasize that any faults in the book are the sole responsibility of the authors, we also stress that this book is the end result of a genuine team effort, drawing upon the expertise and experience of our colleagues from across Europe.

During the three years of the DISCUS project, we have been privileged to be part of the DISCUS team, comprising:

- Stefan Kuhn, Gino van Begin, Naomi Luhde-Thompson and Sarah Lahmani (ICLEI – Local Governments for Sustainability, European Secretariat, Freiburg, Germany: project coordinators);
- Marko Joas, Susan Sundback, Maria Nordström and Tove Måtar (Åbo Akademi University, Åbo, Finland: project partner);
- Joao Farinha (Universidade Nova de Lisboa, Lisbon, Portugal: project partner);
- Walter Sancassiani (Focus Lab, Modena, Italy: project partner);
- Bob Evans and Kate Theobald (Sustainable Cities Research Institute, Northumbria University, Newcastle upon Tyne, UK);
- Lucy Young and Ken Webster (WWF-UK, Godalming, Surrey: project partner);
- Anthony Payne (European Sustainable Cities and Towns Campaign, Brussels, Belgium: consultation partner);
- Agata Miazga (Regional Environmental Centre, Szentendre, Hungary: consultation partner).

Their support and friendship throughout this project is most gratefully acknowledged.

The DISCUS project was fortunate to have the support of an academic Advisory Board who provided valuable comment on the research programme and the analysis. Our thanks go to Katarina Eckerberg (Umea University, Sweden), Rudy Lewanski (University of Bologna, Italy) and Yvonne Rydin (London School of Economics, UK). We were also able to consult sustainability practitioners through our Panel of Practitioners in five local authorities: Mikko Jokinen (Turku/Åbo, Finland), Rita Kellner-Stoll (Bremen, Germany), Jamie Saunders (Bradford, UK), Venelin Donchev Todorov (Bourgas, Bulgaria) and

Katerina Tsakmakidou (Kalithea, Rhodes, Greece). Again, we are most grateful for the time and energy that you all devoted to the project.

For the mammoth task of undertaking the fieldwork in 40 towns and cities across Europe, not to mention the gruelling briefing and de-briefing weekends, we are eternally grateful to our team of fieldworkers who were meticulous in their work and thorough in the presentation of the results. Our thanks go to Katiuscia Fara, Sarah Lahmani, Montserrat Reus-Marti and Silke Moschitz (ICLEI – Local Governments for Sustainability); Ille Allsaar and Mart Reimann (Association of Estonian Cities); Irena Brnada (Regional Environmental Centre, Croatia); Richard Muller (Regional Environmental Centre, Slovakia); Ognyan Enev (Regional Environmental Centre, Bulgaria); Magdalena Chitu (Regional Environmental Centre, Romania); Dalia Gineitiene and Elena Talockaite (ECAT, Lithuania); and Maria Nordström (Åbo Akademi University).

Our thanks go to Sara Lilley and Elaine Ryder of the Sustainable Cities Research Institute of Northumbria University for ensuring the smooth running of the project administration and, in particular, the fieldwork. Thanks also to Sara Lilley, Elaine Ryder and George Dobson for all your help in producing the final manuscript of the book. We extend our thanks to Rob Angell, who worked with the team to set up and run the two internet debates, which provided valuable input as the project progressed.

Our thanks also extend to Brian Brown, scientific officer responsible for the project at the European Commission, who has been unfailingly helpful and supportive through the project.

And, finally, thanks are due to the politicians and officers of the 40 towns and cities who agreed to participate in DISCUS. Without your help, this project could not have been completed. We hope that you will find this book an accurate reflection of your input to the project. Thanks again to everyone who helped and supported us during DISCUS and our apologies to any others whom we have omitted.

Bob Evans, Marko Joas, Susan Sundback and Kate Theobald
October 2004

The DISCUS research project was co-funded by the European Commission's Directorate-General for Research Fifth Framework Programme, 1998–2002, Thematic Programme: Energy, Environment and Sustainable Development, Key Action: 'City of Tomorrow and Cultural Heritage', Contract Number EVK-4-2001-00103.

List of Acronyms and Abbreviations

API	Associazione Piccole e Medie Imprese
DISCUS	Developing Institutional and Social Capacities for Urban Sustainability
DUC	Dunkerque Urban Community
EC	European Community
ECAT	Environmental Centre for Administrative Technology, Lithuania
EIA	environmental impact assessment
EMAS	Environmental Management and Audit Scheme
EU	European Union
ICLEI	International Council for Local Environmental Initiatives
IFOC	local employment agency for sustainable development jobs (Spain)
ISO	International Standards Organization
KLIMP	Nordic Climate Alliance
LA21	Local Agenda 21
LASALA	Local Authorities' Self-Assessment of Local Agenda 21
NGO	non-governmental organization
OECD	Organisation for Economic Co-operation and Development
REC	Regional Environmental Centre
SD	sustainable development
SDP	Social Democratic Party of Germany
SEKO	Swedish eco-municipality network
SME	small and medium-sized enterprise
SPSS	statistical package for social scientists
SUSCOM	Sustainable Communities in Europe
UBC	Union of Baltic Cities
UDS	*Urban Development Strategy* (Munich)
UNDP	United Nations Development Programme
UNESCO	United Nations Educational, Scientific and Cultural Organization
WSSD	World Summit on Sustainable Development

Chapter 1

'The Level of Governance Closest to the People...'

> Because so many of the problems and solutions being addressed by Agenda 21 have their roots in local activities, the participation and cooperation of local authorities will be a determining factor in fulfilling its objectives... As the level of governance closest to the people, they play a vital role in educating, mobilizing and responding to the public to promote sustainable development (United Nations, 1992).

This book is about local government and sustainability, and, crucially, it is concerned with understanding how the first can help to deliver the second. More specifically, it is about cities and towns: the need to create more 'sustainable cities' reflects the fact that the world's population is increasingly an urban one, and that in Europe, in particular, the majority of citizens now live in urban areas. Cities are the source of most of our pollution; they consume our non-renewable raw materials; they have substantial ecological footprints – requiring vast areas of land to provide the food, energy, water and natural resources to keep them operating; and, as centres of population, they contain vast disparities between wealth and poverty.

But cities are clearly more than this. They are the heart of our civilization, the primary source of wealth and enterprise, places of inspiring architecture and the great centres of learning, culture and politics. Perhaps most importantly, though, cities are the locus for change and innovation in all of these things, the places where new ideas, concepts and political visions are moulded into life. The very existence of cities demonstrates the past achievements of humankind and its potential for the future. As Raymond Williams observed: 'This is what men have built, so often magnificently, and is not everything then possible?' (Williams, 1973). As the city emerged in what is now Europe, so did the political structures and institutions that gave it life and order. The processes of the internal government of Aristotle's Greek polis were not so very different from Machiavelli's Italian city state, which, give or take the question of the extension of the franchise, might be seen to be the precursor of 19th-century Birmingham, Lille or Stockholm. The central point, of course, is that it is impossible to disassociate the geographical form and social structure of the city or town from its government. The two go hand in hand. 'Good' urban government presumably results in successful, prosperous and stable cities, whereas 'poor' government does not, and while these two designations are in themselves highly contentious and difficult to satisfactorily define, it does seem reasonable to assume that both states of affairs are inexorably linked.

GOVERNING SUSTAINABLE CITIES

However, the scope of this book is not quite so ambitious. We are not seeking to define 'good' or 'bad' government. Our task is more specific. We wish to examine the veracity of a proposition that is at the heart of the sustainable development agenda, and implicit to the statement quoted at the start of this chapter, which is that *good governance is a precondition for achieving sustainable development – particularly at the local level.* This proposition naturally raises definitional questions. Apart from those relating to 'good' and 'bad' noted above, a central issue is that of 'governance' – what exactly is meant by this, how can it be conceptualized and, most importantly for this book, does it relate in any meaningful way to tangible shifts in public affairs towards what might be regarded as a more sustainable way of life?

Governance is discussed in greater detail in subsequent chapters; but, first, we need to emphasize that, as the title of this book suggests, we are actually interested in the process of *governing*. By this we mean that governing encapsulates two related and intertwined processes, those of *government* and *governance*.[1] We need to be precise in our use of these terms because, within the wide and extensive discourse of sustainable development, there has been a tendency to suggest that, first, governance is somehow unarguably a 'good thing' and that more of it should be encouraged; second, by implication, that 'government' is somehow less desirable; and, finally, that changes in the processes of local politics and administration can usefully be conceptualized as a continuum moving from government to governance with, as indicated above, a clear assumption that any movement along this continuum towards governance is both progressive and supportive of sustainability. To an extent, these positions reflect the analysis offered by the academic political science community (see, for example, John, 2001; Goss, 2001); but the sustainable development discourse, and the actors operating within it, tend to be more normative in approach. Moreover, there is a tendency within this discourse to conflate government and governance, sometimes using the terms interchangeably. However, as will be seen, for the purposes of this book and the research upon which it is based, it is necessary to be clear that these two processes have distinct identities.

Figure 1.1 illustrates these contrasting interpretations and subsequent chapters provide further explanation of our position. Nevertheless, put simply, we have chosen to regard the sphere of local authority activity, the internal organization of local government, and the legal, financial and political processes therein as *government*. In particular, as will be seen in Chapter 2, we are concerned to assess what we term 'institutional capital': the knowledge, resources, leadership and learning that can make local governments effective and

A. The Traditional/Normative Model: the government – governance continuum

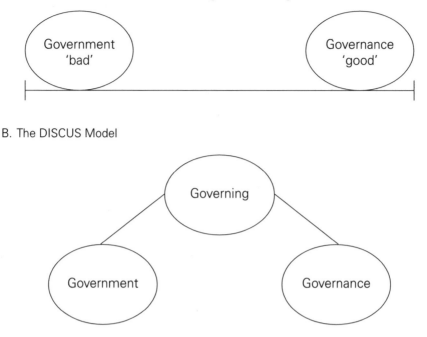

B. The DISCUS Model

Figure 1.1 *Contrasting interpretations of governance*

dynamic entities. *Governance*, on the other hand, is the sphere of public debate, partnership, interaction, dialogue and conflict entered into by local citizens and organizations and by local government. *Governing* is the term that we will use to describe the interaction between these two processes.

In much of the literature reviewing sustainable development, the qualifier 'good' usually, and unnecessarily, precedes 'governance'. For example, the Organisation for Economic Co-operation and Development (OECD, 2002a) asserts that: 'good governance and sound public management are preconditions for the implementation of sustainable development policies', and the UN-Habitat and Global Development Research Centre websites both seek to define and outline the principles of 'good' governance (www.unhabitat.org; www.gdrc. org). Unsurprisingly, there is no generally agreed definition of governance; but there are common points of departure, which are reflected in the final choice of words comprising the many definitions. Thus, governance for an international organization is:

> ...the sum of the many ways [in which] individuals and institutions, public and private, plan and manage the common affairs of the city. It is a continuing process through which conflicting or diverse interests may be accommodated and cooperative action taken (UN-Habitat, 2002).

This contrasts with academic interpretations, where governance is:

> ...a flexible pattern of public decision-making based on loose networks of individuals. The concept conveys the idea that public decisions rest less within hierarchically organized bureaucracies, but take place more in long-term relationships between key individuals located in a diverse set or organizations located at various territorial levels (John, 2001, p9).

Or governance is:

> ...crucially about politics, both formal and informal... [it describes] emerging forms of collective decision-making at [the] local level, which lead to the development of different relationships, not simply between public agencies but between citizens and public agencies (Goss, 2001, p11).

As the title of this chapter suggests, within the sustainable development discourse, governance is central to sustainable development; in particular, it is *local* governance and the search for *local* sustainability that is central to this book. The quotation at the beginning of this chapter is from the document enigmatically known as Agenda 21, and it was this that was instrumental in laying the foundations for what can only be described as a massive shift in governmental attitudes and practice towards the environment in Europe and worldwide over the last decade. Agenda 21 was the 'global action plan' for sustainable development that was agreed at the 1992 Earth Summit held in Rio de Janeiro, and Local Agenda 21 (LA21) was the mechanism that emerged as the means of implementing much of this plan. The rationale behind this brief (less than three-page) document was simple. The changes implied in a move towards more sustainable societies are so immense that governments alone cannot impose them. Change of the magnitude envisaged by Agenda 21 can only be achieved by mobilizing the energy, creativity, knowledge and support of local communities, stakeholders, interest organizations and citizens across the world. More open, deliberative processes, which facilitate the participation of civil society in making decisions, will be required to secure this involvement.

Chapter 28 of Agenda 21, 'Local Authorities' Initiatives in Support of Agenda 21', outlines the objectives of LA21 and the actions required. In particular, local authorities should enter a dialogue with their citizens, local organizations and private enterprises and adopt a Local Agenda 21. Through consensus and consultation, local authorities should learn from citizens and local organizations; in turn, this process of dialogue and consultation should increase local awareness of sustainability. Furthermore, local governments should foster partnerships with other organizations in order to both mobilize support and to promote knowledge and local capacity.

All of this may be broadly conceived as a process of local *governance* – local authorities reaching out to learn, to promote knowledge and understanding, to promote dialogue, and to mobilize resources and energy, and through these activities to generate policies and public actions that will receive consent and support. It is this relationship between civil society and government, this process of governance, which is the focus of the book. However, in making this statement, and as indicated above, we are also clearly differentiating governance from government. As the discussion above has emphasized, the key agency for initiating change is local government itself, and as the history of LA21 in Europe over the last decade has clearly shown, very little would have happened without the energy, leadership and commitment of local government politicians and officials (Evans and Theobald, 2001, 2003). Local governments can exercise legitimate authority – legal, financial and political – within their defined geographical spheres. They can regulate, control, invest and promote within their legal and political remit and responsibilities; with effective leadership, both political and administrative, they may achieve objectives well beyond their formal duties. These achievements may only be realized through consultation, dialogue and participation (the process of governance); but in most cases this will only happen if there is also effective *government*. As will be seen in subsequent chapters, one key element in government is what we refer to as *institutional capital* or *institutional capacity* – the organizational, knowledge and leadership resources of local governments, the possession of which may be a motor for change.

To summarize, this book is about the process of *governing* sustainable cities, and the central theme that runs through the following chapters is that this process of governing may be understood as comprising the two interrelated but distinct sub-processes of *government* and *governance*, and the ways in which these might interact to support (or for that matter undermine) a local process of sustainable development. We are interested in the ways in which local governments interact with those who are often generalized as 'stakeholders', although in reality this term covers a diverse grouping of citizens, local interest groups, non-governmental organizations (NGOs), major employers and landowners, and others who may or may not have a 'stake' in the locality and its future. The research upon which this book is based has investigated these two processes in cities across Europe and has examined the relationship between them and the impact that this has upon achieving sustainable development.

SUSTAINABLE CITIES IN EUROPE

At the time of writing, in June 2004, approximately 5000 local governments across Europe had some kind of local sustainable development process in operation, around 2300 local governments had signed the Aalborg Charter committing themselves to the fundamental principles of sustainable development, and around 1000 delegates had met in Aalborg, Denmark, in June 2004 to reaffirm the Aalborg Charter Principles and to agree and sign the Aalborg Commitments, specifying 'concrete actions' to be undertaken to secure more sustainable lifestyles and policies in their municipalities. Much of this work has been undertaken under the umbrella of the European Sustainable Cities and Towns Campaign (otherwise known as the Campaign), supported by the European Commission and European local government networks, and it is clear that the Campaign and networks such as the International Council for Local Environmental Initiatives (ICLEI), Eurocities, the Climate Alliance and others have been extremely influential in disseminating good practice and knowledge, and supporting European local governments in their sustainability work (Evans and Theobald, 2001; Joas et al, 2001).

While it is clear that many, if not most, European towns and cities are still largely 'unsustainable' (however this might be defined), the changes that have occurred in Europe since the Rio Earth Summit in 1992 are quite remarkable. The European Union (EU) has adopted a Sustainable Development Strategy that is intended to permeate all policies, and while there is a degree of variation across the European Community (EC), there is an increasing number of towns and cities that have actively pursued policies designed to make their localities more sustainable. An indication of the kind of policies and approaches that have been implemented can be derived from the Aalborg Commitments agreed at the June 2004 Fourth European Conference on Sustainable Cities and Towns in Aalborg, Denmark (see Box 1.1). At the end of the conference, 110 cities signed the commitments, and a further 60 indicated their intention to sign in the near future. By signing the commitments, local governments agree to a programme of targets under the headings presented in Box 1.1.

Box 1.1 *The Ten Aalborg Commitments*

1 *Governance*: local governments pledge to increase citizens' participation and cooperation with all spheres of governance in their efforts to become more sustainable.
2 *Urban management*: local governments pledge to formulate, implement and evaluate management schemes aimed at improving urban sustainability.
3 *Natural common goods*: local governments pledge to preserve natural common goods.
4 *Responsible consumption*: promote sustainable consumer habits.
5 *Planning and design*: urban planning is vital in addressing environmental, social, economic and health issues.
6 *Better mobility*: promote sustainable transport.
7 *Local action for health*: local governments have a duty to protect the health of their citizens.
8 *Sustainable local economy*: signatories are committed to creating a vibrant local economy that promotes employment without damaging the environment.
9 *Social equity and justice*: secure inclusive and supportive communities.
10 *Local to global*: signatories pledge to improve sustainability beyond the European Union (EU).

There have been a number of studies of the development of local sustainability initiatives in Europe, primarily focusing upon A21. Of these, the most comprehensive is the transnational Sustainable Communities in Europe (SUSCOM, a cross-national assessment of the implementation of Agenda 21 at the local level) research project reported in Lafferty and Eckerberg (1998) and Lafferty (2001). This work examined the emergence and development of LA21 and similar initiatives across the then 15 European nations, first documenting progress, and subsequently providing an analysis of this in terms of the national contexts and the legal and financial conditions of local governments. This study has provided a unique and valuable insight into the key variables that have determined and conditioned progress across Europe.

The Local Authorities' Self-Assessment of Local Agenda (LASALA) project (Evans and Theobald, 2003) involved a self-assessment exercise with 230 local governments across Europe, examining progress with their LA21 and local sustainability process, including the role of citizens and stakeholders. The research demonstrated the significant levels of commitment to the LA21 process among European local government, and some notable achievements during a very short space of time. The research concluded that although there is still a long way to go, LA21 and the process of governance implicit in this comprise an effective policy vehicle for encouraging and supporting sustainability at the local level in Europe.

These studies have provided valuable insights and a wealth of information on local sustainability in Europe, but they have not sought to investigate the processes of governance and government for sustainability. In particular, these studies did not investigate the relationship between achieving sustainability and the process of governance. This was the central research question for the Developing Institutional and Social Capacities for Urban Sustainability (DISCUS) research programme to which we now turn.

THE DISCUS PROJECT

The DISCUS research programme was funded by the European Commission and was conducted over a three-year period (2001–2004). Eight partners from across Europe undertook an in-depth investigation of local sustainability policy and practice in 40 European cities. As indicated above, the starting point for the research was the fundamental assumption deeply embedded in the 'new sustainability agenda' that emerged from the 1992 Rio Earth Summit – namely, that *good governance is a necessary precondition for achieving sustainable development, particularly at the local level*. This, in turn, led to the principal project research question: *What are the factors and conditions that permit good governance for sustainable urban development?*

The principal research question led, in turn, to three further questions that were to guide the research work:

1   What constitutes 'success' in urban sustainable development policy and practice?

2   What are the factors and conditions that permit or obstruct 'success' in local sustainable development policy and practice?
3   What constitutes 'good governance' for urban sustainable development?

These questions are examined further in subsequent chapters.

The research was based upon case studies of 40 European towns and cities (see Figure 1.2). Thirty of these cities were drawn from a group who had demonstrated their advanced standing in local sustainability in that they were either past winners of the European Sustainable Cities and Towns Award, or they had been identified as 'good practice' cases in the LASALA research noted above. These cities were selected on the basis that they had achieved tangible results and had some kind of active governance process for sustainability, such as an LA21 programme. They could be expected to be useful cases for exploring the research questions outlined above. In contrast, the remaining ten cities were chosen as a control group. As far as the project team could ascertain, these cities had no programme for local sustainability, no known LA21 process and no membership of the Campaign or other networks.

In each city, researchers conducted an analysis of relevant documents, undertook interviews with key respondents from local government and civil society, and conducted a survey questionnaire again with local government and civil society representatives. The case study surveys were supported by an extensive literature review, a review of capacity-building in Europe, contributions from an academic advisory board and a panel of practitioners, as well as two internet debates at the beginning and towards the end of the research. Full details of the research process and the methodology employed can be found in Appendix A; but at this point it is important to explain that in addition to the criteria outlined above, the case study cities were selected to ensure a geographical spread across the EU, including the member states who joined in 2004 and some candidate countries. In order to structure this process, the project team chose to work with a broad division of Europe into four regions: Western, Southern, Northern and Eastern. The purpose of these, admittedly fairly imprecise and arbitrary, divisions was to, first, ensure that the case studies were geographically dispersed so that in the case of the 30 'good practice' studies, the Nordic and western European countries would not be over-represented. Second, there was a need to ensure that there was consideration of the different local government contexts and traditions exhibited across Europe.

Throughout the remainder of this book, reference is made to these four regions, and at various points, data from the survey work are presented on a regional basis. However, it is important to emphasize that these regions have been defined simply as heuristic devices in order to structure the research process and to simplify the presentation of results at key points. The regions as defined have no political, legal, cultural, policy or economic coherence and there is no intention to ascribe such characteristics to them.

DISCUS

Developing Institutional
and Social Capacities
for Urban Sustainability

40 participating cities

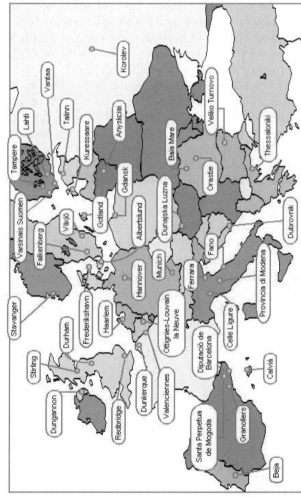

Figure 1.2 *Map of the 40 participating cities*

Source: ICLEI

THE CHAPTERS

The remaining chapters in the book report on the DISCUS research. Chapter 2 outlines the theoretical context for the report, evaluating the concepts that are central to the book's key themes – notably, institutional capacity, social capacity and capacity-building as they pertain to the sustainable development policy discourse. The chapter also presents a matrix of potential governing arrangements for sustainable development that underpin the evaluations contained in subsequent chapters.

Chapters 3, 4 and 5 outline the empirical material that was collected during the research, and assess and evaluate this evidence in order to address the key questions outlined earlier. Chapter 3 outlines the development of urban sustainability policy and practice in Europe as the context for the research findings on progress in the 40 case study cities. The key theme of this chapter is the assessment of policy 'achievement' at the local level.

Chapter 4 assesses the evidence from the survey work on institutional capacity, social capacity and capacity-building for sustainable development. Drawing upon the theoretical background outlined in Chapter 2, the chapter examines the factors that might underpin or prevent the development of local capacity for sustainability. The final empirical chapter, Chapter 5, considers the processes of governance and government in the 40 cities, reflecting upon how organized interests in civil society and local government perceive their relationship in the arena of sustainability.

The final two chapters contain the main conclusions of the research. Chapter 6 brings together the themes from the empirical findings and provides a series of conclusions and responses to the research questions. This chapter also proposes a theoretical model of institutional and social capacities for urban sustainability and provides a revised matrix of governing arrangements. On the basis of the research findings, Chapter 7 provides guidelines for future policy action at local, national and European levels.

NOTE

1   We are indebted to Harriet Bulkeley of Durham University, UK, for alerting us to this conceptual insight.

Chapter 2

Government, Governance and Local Sustainability

INTRODUCTION

This chapter outlines the theoretical and conceptual underpinnings of the Developing Institutional and Social Capacities for Urban Sustainability (DISCUS) research, and provides the context for subsequent chapters. As was explained in Chapter 1, our central concern in this book is to investigate the process of governing for sustainability, which may be understood as comprising the two interrelated processes of government and governance. These refer, respectively, to the role and capacity of, in this case, local government, and to the ways in which local government interacts with actors in civil society. In order to undertake this investigation, we need to clarify the concepts involved and the interaction between them. However, in drawing upon the existing literature and research evidence, it is clear that the guiding paradigm in virtually all cases is one where 'governance' is used to describe the process that we are choosing to call 'governing' – that is, the processes of government and governance, which for us are conceptually distinct, are conflated into one by many analysts.

In this chapter we examine the conceptual underpinnings of the DISCUS research and conclude the discussion with an analytical model that takes our empirical research task further. Before presenting the analytical model we introduce the reader to the normative and theoretical discussions on ('good') governance and governing, social capital, institutional capital and capacity-building within both of these spheres of activity. We also introduce the reader to a discussion of what could be considered as 'success' in sustainable development policy outcomes.

WHAT IS 'GOOD' GOVERNANCE?

The normative dimension of the term is clear and, particularly in the sustainable development literature, is dominant. Governance is used in a normative manner to describe a move towards a process where the formal institutions of government enter into a dialogue about the policy process with actors from civil society. Thus, it is argued, more collaborative, consensual and democratic ways of working emerge that are more 'bottom up' in nature, compared with the traditional processes of government, which tend to be 'top down' and relatively unconcerned about involving civil society actors in the policy process. However, like so many other terms and concepts that have a significant normative dimension, once this is stripped away, definition and analysis are less clear. The concept carries a high level of ambiguity and it is not altogether obvious that a clear dividing line may be drawn between the processes of government, on the one hand, and those of governance, on the other.

In part, this is because it is impossible to conceive of either notion in a political or power vacuum. For example, the classical Marxist understanding of the state holds that it is 'but a committee for managing the affairs of the whole bourgeoisie'. The formal machinery of *government* is utilized by the dominant class in society to further its own ends. There might be some 'relative autonomy' – the institutions and functionaries of the state may from time to time make and take decisions that are not in the best interests of capital; but, fundamentally, according to this line of argument, government must be understood as class rule.

Regardless of whether this particular analysis is accepted, the crucial point is that the processes of public decision-making – whether this is described as government or governance – are conducted in the context of the social, economic and political relations of the particular society in question. It is impossible to divorce the institutions and their 'ways of working' from this wider context. Calls for governance are therefore not merely demands for different ways of taking decisions. They are also likely to represent more substantial demands for greater access to power and resources by those currently excluded.

However, there is another side to this. Governance may also be regarded as a response to the changing circumstances of power relations in a move to secure more reflexive modes of public decision-making that can circumvent both market failure and the problems of 'rational-bureaucratic' state action. This view of governance, therefore, sees the process as a necessary adaptation in modes of rule, rather than as a radical realignment of power relations towards those who have historically been excluded.

The European Union (EU) has an established commitment to reform the processes of European governance as presented in *European Governance: A White Paper* (EC, 2001). In this report, a modernization of European governance is seen as a necessary precondition for European integration through a process of decentralization, combating the impact of globalization, and a restoration of faith in democracy through wider involvement in decision-making. The White Paper identifies five principles that underpin good governance – *openness, participation, accountability, effectiveness* and *coherence* – which should apply to all levels of government, from the local to the global.

The White Paper recognizes that the creation of the EU and the challenges of policy in a globalized world necessitate new ways of working that are not possible within a traditional framework of top-down government: 'Policies can no longer be effective unless they are prepared, implemented and enforced in a more inclusive way' (EC, 2001, p18). By implication, the proposal demands a degree of power transference between levels of government (through proportionality and subsidiarity) and from government to civil society. Such transfers of power, responsibility and influence have historically met with opposition from the current holders of power.

Scholars debating governance thus find two major interpretations of the concept. One of the research traditions starts the analysis from a state-centric perspective (that is, playing the old game with new rules), the other one from a social perspective (that is, changing the game altogether). This latter implies a change in existing power relations and, hence, a change in the position of the government in the decision-making process (Pierre, 2000, pp3–4). Following the latter frame of reference, the process of governance – governing – can be defined as:

> ...the totality of interactions, in which public as well as private actors participate, aimed at solving societal problems or creating societal opportunities; attending to the institutions as contexts for these governing institutions; and establishing a normative foundation for all those activities (Kooiman, 2003, p4).

'GOOD' GOVERNANCE AND SUSTAINABLE DEVELOPMENT

The sustainable development discourse places heavy emphasis upon the need to develop more democratic mechanisms for decision-making and policy implementation: 'Governance theory emphasizes "joint" or co-governance by state and non-state actors, and the self-governing capacities of society; hierarchical governance (or government) tends to be de-emphasized by writers who presume "governance"' (Sibeon, 2002, pp16–17).

Governance is seen to be evidenced in a strong and dynamic organization of local government and culture of 'institutional learning'. According to this perspective, political actors need to employ creative intervention in order to change structures. The emerging new hybrid forms of governing 'implies a greater willingness to cope with uncertainty and open-endedness on the part of policy-framers' (Stocker, 2002, p6). In turn, citizens' concerns are assumed to be well informed (that is, based on information and knowledge) and they are perceived to seek better 'performance' from public agencies.

The emphasis on improving democratic mechanisms for decision-making leads to calls for human equity and environmental justice, more effective environmental governance and greater environmental democracy. Christie and Warburton (2001, p154) argue that good governance is central to sustainability:

> The fundamental driver of sustainable development must be democratic debate – decisions reached through open discussion, consensus based on shared goals and trust. Sustainable development needs representative democracy that is trusted and vibrant, and new forms of participatory democracy to complement it that can inspire greater engagement by citizens in creating a better world.

They argue that a renewal of trust in public institutions and of local democracy will be required if the sustainability agenda is to be delivered.

This relationship is already tested empirically, but on a national level. In a comparative study of 30 nations, a research team led by Martin Jänicke has shown that 'democratic structures and procedures in all areas of society, and not only in the political system, are key preconditions for effective environmental policy' (Weidner, 2002, p1363). This requirement should be even more relevant for sustainable development, taking into account the natural cross-sector orientation of this policy area.

UNDERSTANDING 'SOCIAL CAPITAL'

Like many other terms, social capital may be overexposed and, perhaps, too often regarded as a panacea for all social ills. Before discussing the different conceptualizations of social capital, it is necessary to briefly explain our understanding of the term 'civil society', as it is within this sector that social capital, however defined, is developed and maintained. There are many competing conceptualizations of civil society. For the purposes of this research we have chosen to utilize the definition of civil society as all social, economic and political activities that take place outside of local government – that is, in work, employment, local communities and interest organizations. Included in this are business and industry, voluntary and community groups representing the interests of a range of individuals and sectors, and non-governmental organizations (NGOs) from environmental, social and economic arenas.

The complex ways in which these sectors of civil society build and maintain capacity (economic, social and mutual support) for action to promote the needs of different groups is encompassed in the concept of social capital. The concept of social capital has achieved wide usage in social science since it was popularized by Pierre Bourdieu (1986) and James Coleman (1988) during the 1980s. It was further developed by Robert Putnam (1993) (see also Putnam, 2000) and Fukuyama (1995; see also Fukuyama, 2001) during the 1990s, particularly in terms of drawing the concept of social capital into widespread use in academic and policy debates. The concept can be broadly defined as: 'those networks and assets that facilitate the education, coordination and cooperation of citizens for mutual benefit' (Putnam, 1993; see also Van Deth, 2000).

Social capital in this context therefore refers to the *collective* capacity that has been built or exists within a 'community' and within a local context. The production of social capital is argued to relate to more than just the existence of a 'community' or established network of interests. Bourdieu (1986), for instance, looks at the routine practices of everyday life or what he terms the 'weak ties' that are the subtler associations between people that facilitate and sustain social advantage (or disadvantage). These 'weak ties' could include trust and reciprocity between individuals in informal ways (not necessarily within the setting of a group or organization). For Bourdieu, social capital was underpinned by *economic capital*, and more recent commentators such as Putnam (1993) and Skidmore (2001) reinforce this point. Skidmore (2001) argues that social capital inheres in the organizational features of social and economic life. It is explicitly relational and cannot be produced by individuals acting in isolation from one another.

Putnam (2000), in a more recent conceptualization of social capital, makes an important distinction between what he terms 'bridging (inclusive) social capital' and 'bonding (exclusive) social capital'. Bonding social capital is good for 'getting by'. This understanding relates to, perhaps, the 'weak ties' that Bourdieu (1986) refers to, such as the bonds and associations at an individual level that link people together. However, bridging social capital is crucial for 'getting ahead' – that is, making links between groups/organizations in a more collective and cooperative sense. Thus, Putnam sees bonding social capital as 'sociological superglue' and bridging social capital as 'sociological WD40'. He does note, however, that the two are not interchangeable, although the differences between them are also unclear. A similar distinction has been made by Taylor (2000), who differentiates between 'communal' and 'collaborative' social capital, and 'community capacity'.

Rydin and Holman (2004), reflecting on social capital in the context of sustainable development, propose an extension of Putman's categories by suggesting a third, that of 'bracing' social capital:

> ...we have coined the term 'bracing' social capital to capture the idea of a kind of social capital that is primarily concerned [with strengthening] links across and between scales and sectors, but only operates within a limited set of actors. It provides a kind of social scaffolding (Rydin and Holman, 2004, p123).

Brown and Lauder (2000) locate the concept of social capital in a broader framework of what they term the 'struggle for collective intelligence'. The development of a conceptual framework of 'collective intelligence' is necessary for the reconstruction of social solidarity. This collective intelligence comes about through one having knowledge of one's own position, but also of that of others. Collective intelligence can be defined as empowerment through the development and pooling of intelligence to attain common goals or resolve common problems.

The authors make a useful distinction between the 'capacity for intelligence' and 'relations of trust'. The former includes the state of knowledge, technology and intellectual resources upon which societies can draw. The latter relates to the ways in which the nature and distribution of intelligence will be shaped, both by social groups to which an individual belongs, and by the cultural, economic and political institutions of society. For Brown and Lauder (2000), the interrelationship between *capacities* and *relations* is vital because it is within the nexus between these two that the 'space' or possibilities for individuals to develop their capabilities for intelligent action will be created. This relationship is also about the extent to which people are institutionally encouraged to pool their capacity for intelligent action. The authors argue, therefore, that in post-industrial societies collective intelligence needs to become the 'social glue that holds societies together'.

THE ELEMENTS OF SOCIAL CAPITAL

The key elements of social capital and, related to this, the conditions for social capital as identified by a number of writers are *trust* or *trust relationships*, *reciprocity*, *networks* and *partnerships*, with different commentators according importance to one or a combination of these aspects. Forrest and Kearns (2001) suggest that social capital itself is an important constituent dimension of what they term 'social cohesion'. Linked to social capital are other dimensions of social cohesion – common values and a civic culture, social order, social networks – and all of these aspects interrelate and impact upon each other. Social cohesion here is viewed as a bottom-up process, founded upon local social capital. For Forrest and Kearns, networks are particularly important: in association with civic engagement and community organizations, they are constitutive of, and producers of, social capital.

Putnam (2000) places the issue of trust and reciprocity at the heart of social capital. In a similar vein to Bourdieu's (1986) understanding of social capital, Putnam argues that 'trusting communities' have a measurable economic advantage, and that a society that relies on generalized reciprocity is more efficient than a distrustful one. Putnam employs the related concepts of 'thick trust' (strong personal relations that are embedded in wider networks) and 'thin trust' (which extends to acquaintances and networks) and argues that the latter is even more important than thick trust and is getting rarer. For Putnam, this 'social' or 'thin' trust is associated with many other forms of civic engagement and social capital. He further makes the important point that 'thin trust' is very different from that related to institutions and political authorities. He suggests that trust in government may be a *cause* or *consequence of social trust*; yet it is not the same thing. Trust that exists between sectors of civil society and local government institutions is central to the development of 'bridging social capital'. This may, in turn, impact upon the capacity of municipalities to successfully implement policies for sustainable development.

Social movements and social capital are very closely connected (although it is unclear which is cause and which is effect). For Putnam (2000), social movements both embody and produce social capital and are thus extremely valuable in maintaining stocks of social capital. In terms of measuring civic participation, Putnam considers the role of environmental organizations, and notes that although individuals may be members of such organizations, through regular subscriptions, this 'mail-order membership' is a poor measure of civic engagement. 'Card carrying' membership does not accurately reflect involvement in activities; indeed, Putnam and others point out that someone who 'belongs' to many groups may be active in none. A reduction in civic engagement in this area may have considerable negative implications for the relationship between local governments and civil society in addressing the requirements of urban sustainable development.

The importance of the global civil society and international social movements is also evident within the area of sustainable development. Even though environmental NGOs are not present in every locality, as put by Sonnenfeld and Mol

(2002, p1331), they still play an important role in mainstreaming the normative structures in sustainable development matters, in monitoring international and national-level development and in functioning as information channels.

Purdue (2001) suggests that *networks* containing substantial social capital need to be 'closed' in order to reinforce the capacity that has been built. Closed social networks are essential to develop social capital in a neighbourhood. Yet, in practice, he observes that community networks are in many cases fragmented, rather than closed, thus limiting the capacity to retain social capital. He suggests that ambivalence over trust between individuals and organizations in both partnerships and community reveals difficulties in accumulating social capital.

A working definition of social capital that includes the notions of bridging social capital could therefore include the level of trust; extent of networks; density of relationships within networks; knowledge of relationships; obligations and reciprocity; forms of local knowledge; operating norms; and sanctions to punish free-riding (Rydin and Pennington, 2000).

THE LEVEL AND NATURE OF SOCIAL CAPITAL

The level of social capital has changed considerably over time and place, and in different areas of social and political life. Putnam (2000) argues that at least the recent changes are a function of the change in the nature of citizenship towards a more individualistic notion of citizenship, in line with other views of the post-industrial development of societies (see, for example, Beck, 1986; Giddens, 1991). Putnam suggests one of the reasons for a change in social capital is that *place-based social capital* is being supplanted by *function-based social capital*.

Putnam sees suburbanization as a key factor. Spatial fragmentation between home and the workplace can be seen as detrimental to civic involvement. Urban 'sprawl' disrupts community ties. In addition, Putnam identifies some association between civic disengagement and corporate disengagement through globalization. Furthermore, a larger range of home-based leisure activities, as opposed to activities in public space is associated with decreased civic activism and decreased collective activity (Putnam 2000).

Putnam (2000) and Rothstein (2001) both note that the level of social capital is positively correlated with the size of government – that is, the larger the scale of government or the greater the involvement of the public sector in areas of social life, the greater the existence of trust between civil society and government institutions. As a general trend, however, public participation in formal political activity is declining across modern Western democracies. Putnam notes, for example, that in 1973 most Americans engaged in at least one form of civic involvement each year. By 1994, most did not engage in any civic activities. In relation to Sweden, Rothstein notes that, in terms of political participation (time spent in established forms of political activity), there have been two opposing trends. There is an increasing interest in politics; but this interest is less in traditional channels and more towards 'one-issue' organizations.

'Cooperative' forms of behaviour have declined more rapidly than 'expressive' forms. Clearly Putnam's findings refer to the experience in the US. However, they are also applicable, to some degree, within European countries.

Rydin and Pennington (2000) argue that building social capital is seen as a way of changing the pattern of incentives in order to overcome collective action problems – through trust-building, sanctions, strengthening of relationships and involvement to reinforce social identity/values. Putnam (2000) extends this list further, arguing that social capital allows communities to advance smoothly in political, social and economic terms, and that it widens awareness of how the experiences and 'fates' of individuals are linked.

For Putnam (2000), the existence of social capital is closely tied in with the effective functioning of a democracy. Voluntary associations provide opportunities for learning civic virtues – the relevance of active participation in public life, trustworthiness and reciprocity – even if there are empirical studies that indicate that no direct link exists between traditional political participation (electoral turn-out) and social capital (associational activity) (Lundåsen, 2004). Effective democracy can occur, instead, through representative organizations or stakeholder groups, putting forward the needs and concerns of the individuals whom they represent. Civic engagement matters equally on the demand side – civil society expecting better government – and on the supply side (the performance of representative government is facilitated by the social infrastructure of civic communities and of officials and citizens). The interrelationship between the 'demand' and 'supply' sides is thus directly affected both by the nature and levels of social capital within sectors of civil society. It is also affected by the ways in which governments (of all levels) support and encourage the development of social capital.

Furthermore, communities who possess high levels of social capital will experience higher levels of economic performance and social welfare (Putnam, 1993; Skidmore, 2001). A high level of social capital is clearly beneficial for social development, in general. The existence of, and support for, social capital is a 'good thing'. However, it is appropriate to consider that the benefits of social capital can be less clear cut in some instances. Putnam (2000) argues that generalized reciprocity is beneficial for those within networks; but, for example, *power elites* may exploit these ties to achieve ends that are negative from wider social perspectives.

SOCIAL CAPITAL AND LOCAL SUSTAINABLE DEVELOPMENT

A clear reason for an interest by policy-makers in the notion of social capital is the revival in the ideas of 'local community' (Etzioni, 1993), and this has been applied particularly in policies that aim to tackle area deprivation and social exclusion. The principal assumption here is that neighbourhood decline sets in train a cumulative decline in social capital. Forrest and Kearns (2000, 2001) explore how the concepts of urban dynamics and governance fit into debates on social cohesion, and suggest that in considering the possible links between urban governance and social cohesion it is necessary to also look at three spatial levels: interurban, city and city-region, and neighbourhood. The problems of cities (and particularly poorer areas within these) are traditionally at the heart of current concerns about social cohesion. The emphasis in urban policy-making has thus tended to be on *privilege* rather than disadvantage, and on what disadvantaged areas may lack rather than on what apparently successful neighbourhoods may possess. However, this approach to policy-making does not directly address the issue of the forms of social capital that 'successful' communities possess.

Purdue (2001) suggests that social capital, consisting of trust relationships between a community and its leaders (referred to as 'social entrepreneurs') can contribute to the effectiveness of neighbourhood regeneration partnerships. Purdue argues that successful partnerships in this policy area depend upon these community leaders acting as community representatives. If this is the case, then it would appear that community leaders (whether from civil society or from local government) have a key role to play in the development and maintenance of high levels of social capital.

Only a limited amount of research on the nature of social capital as applied to local environmental decision-making processes exists. Rydin and Pennington (2000), writing on the nature of social capital within decision-making processes on the local environment, question the usefulness of the concept of social capital in relation to 'trust', and argue that relations of trust can only be usefully applied within a specific social and political context. Social capital defined in terms of trust can only therefore be usefully applied in relation to individuals and organizations involved in a specific environmental collective action problem and the extent to which the relevant trust constitutes an element within the prevailing incentive structure. Furthermore, they suggest that the existence of networks of individuals and organizations cannot of itself be considered as evidence of social capital. 'Networks' describe the structure of specific policy communities, but do not explain why the structures function in the way they do. Thus, it is important to study these in the context of the political and institutional arrangements of which they are a part.

Rydin and Holman (2004) suggest that social capital can contribute to sustainable development in a number of ways, but argue that it is important to recognize that the different types of social capital perform different functions. However, they recognize that the question of how to actually support or generate such capital is, as yet, unresolved. A key question in this context is whether patterns of policy networks (in the environmental or sustainable development policy arena) are simply reflective of underlying collective action problems or whether the presence or absence of social capital has affected the character of these networks. Rydin and Pennington (2000) suggest that often in NGO activity, it falls on committed individuals to aid survival of the group – they refer to these people as 'environmental entrepreneurs'. Nevertheless, it also depends on the policy area and the capacity of NGOs to stimulate collective action within their groups.

Two particular conceptualizations are of specific relevance to this project: the notion of 'bridging social capital', as identified by Putnam (2000, p22), and, linked to this, the concept of 'collaborative social capital'. The focus is therefore on the conditions for networks and groups in civil society to be 'outward looking' in engaging with other groups, and with local government. A key factor in this appears to be the existence of social relations of 'trust' both within networks, and between civil society and local government. In this sense, we are moving away from the notion of social capital in terms of social/family ties to more 'formal' modes of engagement in society.

Many of the terms associated with the notion of social capital have resonance with involving different sectors of civil society in decision-making processes, and creating the conditions where stakeholder groups feel that their views and concerns are adequately considered and incorporated. Arguably, social capital needs to exist for stakeholders to feel that they do have a stake in, and an impact upon, decision-making processes for sustainable development policy formulation and implementation. Linked to ideas of social capital are the mechanisms that exist within civil society for *capacity-building* (either 'bottom up' or supported by local government). The terms 'participation' and 'partnership' are commonly used in policy rhetoric on the shift to 'governance'. Yet, there is often an underlying assumption that these are 'right' and 'good' and represent a more democratic approach to policy-making.

This discussion of social capital provides us with a context within which we can locate our evaluation of governance as part of a wider process of governing. However, it must be emphasized that the DISCUS project did not seek to research levels of social capital in the 40 case study cities. It was possible to make generalized assessments as to levels of civic engagement – for example, in terms of local pressure group activity; but the project could not, and did not intend to, undertake detailed research into levels of social capital, however defined, within the cities studied.

Understanding 'institutional capital'

The concept of *social capital* is generally argued to be highly relevant to describe the long-term trends in the capacities of societies to function within the boundaries of the political system. Central theorists within this tradition (for example, Coleman, 1988, and Putnam, 1993, 2000) often neglect the governmental input to this process. Lowndes and Wilson (2001, p629) argue that the work by Putnam is simply: 'too society centred, under-valuing state agency and associated political factors'.

However, it is a commonly held view that sustainable development – with cross-cutting objectives over several policy sectors – can only be achieved with common capacity-building efforts by civil society and local government, as well as by other local public-sector authorities. Societal processes of involving new agents in the (local) policy-making process are interpreted very differently according to whether the observer has a state-centric view or a society-oriented view. The 'shift' from government to governance – the definition of this 'shift' is highly contended – has been identified with labels as negative as '*the hollowing out of the state*', as well as positive-sounding '*empowerment of the people*' (see, for example, Rhodes, 1996, and Selman, 1996). This change in the role of the nation state as a political authority is an evident feature in most of the Western states. This development is evident in environmental and sustainability policies; a simultaneous movement of political power can be noticed both up to transnational levels of government and down to the local communities (Joas, 2001, p232). In addition, this seems to apply in relation to non-governmental agents such as civic organizations and even loosely constructed networks (Dryzek, 1997; Gibbs, 2000). To redirect political powers in this way lies, perhaps, at the heart of the problems of sustainability. Global problems are seen as problems hanging between two spheres of society; therefore, both local and global efforts have to be implemented in order to reach any meaningful results.

In political and other social sciences, the concept of 'institution' is very broad. The new institutional analyses define 'society as a game and institutions as the rules that guide the game' (Hukkinen, 1999, p3). Institutions are thus a set of formal and informal rules and patterns of behaviour that define the activities of a certain group of people. Institutions can be formal and tightly structured and defined by other institutions – for example, a national assembly – or very informal and only loosely or partly defined by the rest of the society – for example, a family. Defined in a similar way, the *internal patterns of behaviour and ways of working, as well as the collective values, knowledge and relationships that exist within any organized group in society*, can be termed *institutional capital*. This means that the term covers, as noted also by Healey et al (2002), intellectual capital, social capital and political capital, the latter being defined as the capacity to act collectively.

These processes can be both steered and non-steered by government; they can thus include planned and unplanned capacity-building efforts both within local government, as well as within local civil society. There is no single, perfect solution for all circumstances. 'Institutional capital', as well as 'social capital', are thus 'evaluative and normative concepts', while referring to the 'richness that enables individuals and groups to mobilize resources and perform meaningful action' (Madanipour, 2002, p4). It is highly significant to note that this kind of new institutional capital is perceived to be created especially within the sphere of sustainability policies. What is not clear is whether this is just a case of an institutionalization of a rather new, young policy sector, or does this policy sector include elements that especially enable this development?

THE INTERPLAY BETWEEN SOCIAL CAPITAL AND INSTITUTIONAL CAPITAL

The conceptual definitions of phenomena close to institutional capital vary depending upon the research topic. Debates of interest to this research include those that focus on concepts such as institutional design, ecological modernization, capacity-building and institutional learning. Authors such as Lowndes and Wilson (2001) emphasize, for example, the role played by *institutional design* by governments, a relevant notion especially within a newly institutionalized policy field, such as sustainability policies. Maloney et al (2000) instead call upon a clearer acknowledgement of the local government role in the *creation* and *function* of social capital. Furthermore, Rothstein (2001, p207) notes that social capital can, in fact, 'be caused by how government institutions operate and not by voluntary associations'.

Close cooperation between the state and organized interests has always been a visible feature of the consensus-oriented Nordic countries, and this is a democratic feature that one would not assume to be compatible with a strong civil society, at least according to the traditional theorists within this field. Yet, Rothstein (2001) concludes his argument and empirical analysis with the finding that the Swedish civil society is vital, growing and still changing, despite the extensive involvement in civil society by the social democratic government.

Traditionally, in democratic societies, political structures have been stable. In a classic work by David Easton, political systems are defined as 'those interactions through which values are authoritatively allocated for a society' (Easton, 1965, p21). Society is thus accustomed to the fact that there are formal institutions to take care of the allocation of values, resources and rules. These institutions are, however, dynamic. One key aspect in democratic political systems is that they have the capacity to respond to crises and political upheaval and, therefore, also have the ability to adapt themselves to changes in the political environment, whether these changes are physical or societal (Easton, 1965). The introduction of environmental and sustainability concerns to the political agenda has clearly put the traditional political systems based on representative democracy under stress. But empirical studies show that, even though the procedures of representative democracy are adapting following the sustainable development and ecological modernization processes, the policy achievements are still clearly ahead of other forms of governing systems. This is a result of the high-level institutional adaptability that democratic systems possess (Weidner, 2002).

This approach is useful to consider, as institutional capital includes both the government, as well as the governance aspects of the political sphere of activity. In our research we are limiting ourselves to use the concept only in relation to (local) government activities – that is, activities within the local government and local authorities, or together with the civil society.

During the last 30 years, national governments in all Western European countries have invested in the development of institutional capital – capacity-building – within the sphere of *environmental policy-making*. The creation of a new policy sector was especially evident during the early years of the 1970s. According to Jänicke (1997), differences in this basic environmental capacity – institutional capital – explain to a certain degree differences in environmental policy outcomes between industrialized countries. Even if sustainable development is seen as one core feature in the process of ecological modernization of the contemporary society, it is not yet clear how the latest changes will affect existing institutions. Ecological modernization theory expects, in general, however, that existing political structures should be able to handle the change. Existing political institutions, as well as specialized administrative institutions, should be able to internalize ecological concerns into everyday policy processes (Hajer,

1996). Thus, the leading role of the state is not fundamentally questioned, and the 'hollowing-out' processes with a greater role for the market and other decentralized political solutions simply introduce new forms of governance, which do not replace those structures already in place. Several empirical analyses indicate that institutions have rather been adapted, and only partly (re)created, within the sphere of national governments in order to (re)gain the control of environmental and sustainability policy processes (Young, 2000; Joas, 2001; Lundqvist, 2001).

The process of ecological modernization does not only apply for nation states. It seems clear that the traditional structures will adjust themselves to the change, and this seems to be the case also at the local level. The environmental policy capacity-building process at the local level can also be seen as central to achieving environmental goals at the local government level (Joas, 2001, p244).

As a simplified analytical definition of institutional capital we use the following: *institutional capital includes basic monetary and human resources, existing and working structures and networks within (local) government, as well as with organized interests and individuals outside the government.* This kind of capital can be created, further developed or dismantled. It has a higher value and degree of efficiency than any single actor – organization or individual – within it.

INSTITUTIONAL CAPACITY-BUILDING

There are at least two different terms for a process that aims to enhance and improve the basic resources of an institution (financial, human, time, ways of working) to handle a certain problem or area of action. Depending to some degree upon the type of resources included in the process, we can either refer to the concept of *institutional/organizational learning*, or *institutional/organizational capacity-building*.

The process of institutional learning refers more to processes that indicate the ways in which new ideas become established within governmental and other institutions or organizations. However, for the purposes of this study we are using the concept of institutional capacity-building as we would expect to find in our analysis more formal institutions being created than just the introduction of new concepts or ideas.

Capacity-building has clearly been one of the central notions in the sustainability agenda since the introduction of the concept in the Brundtland Report (WCED, 1987). Capacity-building efforts, on all societal levels, have been advocated in policy rhetoric as both crucial and inevitable for a sustainable future, as was the case in Agenda 21 (Chapter 37):

> The ability of a country to follow sustainable development paths
> is determined to a large extent by the capacity of its people and its
> institutions, as well as by its ecological and geographical conditions.

> Specifically, capacity-building encompasses the country's human,
> scientific, technological, organizational, institutional and resource
> capabilities.

The research team led by Martin Jänicke (see, for example, Jänicke, 1995,
1997; Weidner and Jänicke, 2002) has examined national-level environmental
policy and ecological modernization capacities in a comparative perspective.
In order to achieve good results in environmental policies, several factors must
co-influence each other: 'successful environmental protection is brought about
by a complex interaction of influences and not by a single, isolated factor, nor
favourite instrument, nor a single type of actor, nor a particular framework
condition or institution' (Jänicke, 1997, p4). Jänicke and Weidner (1995) list
five factors that explain environmental policy success:

1 *structures*: political, economic and cultural framework conditions for policy
   action;
2 *situations*: specific situations steer the policy action;
3 *actors*: proponents and opponents of policy action;
4 *strategies*: capacities for planned and oriented policy action; and
5 *time*: important for investment and learning processes.

Environmental policy performance is evidently also influenced by other factors
than structural capacities, but this does not mean that political factors should
be forgotten. Especially in earlier studies, the German school of ecological
modernization stressed the importance of the basic capacities created by the
state, such as an environmental administration sector and other core institutions
with sufficient political support and economic resources: 'By capacity for
modernization we mean the general level of institutional, material and technical
ability in a country to find solutions to problems' (Jänicke, 1995, p32).

The capacities and the level of capacity-building measures that are needed
for a certain problem vary considerably. The trigger for the change process is a
new and higher level of environmental problem pressure and knowledge. To be
able to react at all, a society must have or must create a certain level of economic
capacity and performance, and consensus capacity to handle socio-cultural
conflicts. An existing and fully functional political and administrative system is
also central to this, according to Jänicke (1995). A certain level of institutional
capacity must exist to be able to act accordingly to the changes in the trigger.
In addition, the administrative system should have enough decision-making
resources – that is, competence, staff and material resources, and a certain level
of long-term, open and integrated innovation capacity (see also Joas, 2001).

Jänicke's emphasis on the importance of pre-existing structures, enabling
new action, as well as the general assumption of the impetus created by a well-
functioning network of social capital, is reinforced in other literature. Gualini
(2002) uses the concepts of *institution-building* and *institutional design*. The
former concept emphasizes the 'mobilisation and commitment of individuals
as the foremost way to constitute and develop "collective forms of action"...
into stable institutional patterns' (Gualini, 2002, p35).

The latter concept promotes the ideas that previous institutional arrangements affect the creation of new institutional settings and structures. A useful working definition for general capacity-building is, therefore:

> Institutional capacity-building is seen as eventually emerging as a result of incremental, self-transforming and self-policing processes... Rather, collective action becomes an emergent, incremental outcome that may itself retro-act on the conditions for the constitution of new institutional settings, and thus originate processes of institutional change (Gualini, 2002, p37).

INSTITUTIONAL CAPITAL AND CAPACITY-BUILDING WITHIN LOCAL GOVERNMENT

The scope for cities to act is often narrow; nevertheless, the local-level knowledge and competence is generally recognized to be of central importance (see, for example, Ostrom 2000). For Skinner (1997), the importance of the local level is evident. In his definition of capacity-building for sustainable development he notes that it is capacity-building that gives the ability for stakeholders to build their institutions and skills so they are 'able to define and achieve their objectives and engage in consultation and planning, manage community projects, and take part in partnership and community enterprises'.

Most new political decisions that must be taken into consideration in order to take steps towards sustainability will dramatically impact upon the lives of 'normal' people. This is the case for several reasons.

First of all, environmental policy instruments have so far been utilized more to influence producer rather than consumer behaviour. This has been the 'easier' solution. The number of producers is much smaller than the number of consumers or citizens, and they have been a group that has been an easy target – especially for consensual policy-making efforts. Today, however, much of the environmental policy instruments that exist or are foreseen with modern technologies, and economic and political solutions, are already in use in most of the modern industrialized nations. The behaviour of individuals is, nevertheless, much more difficult to control.

Second, the introduction of direct costs of exchange of values, imposed on individuals, and which will 'only' give in exchange diffuse collective benefits, has never been too popular in democracies. This is especially true regarding sustainability questions that should be seen in a very long time span, and definitely not with an average election period of four to five years. This is one reason for the argument that citizens, as well as politicians, must be 'trained' or educated to adopt the changes in lifestyle and behaviour that sustainable development requires. This process of legitimizing the new policies of sustainability cannot be forced upon local communities within democratic political systems; instead, it is a long-term learning process. As long as much of the everyday processes that are changing belong rather naturally to the sphere of local decision-making, it will only be natural to see local government as the appropriate political level to introduce the 'new policies of sustainability'.

Local government represents the legitimate process of political activity and administration typical of most European societies. We are fully aware of the fact that the political powers and statuses, the range of issues, the economic resources for political action, as well as the modes of public representation vary considerably between states, and also between different types of local government within nation states. Local government may be wholly or partially an instrument of the state, and therefore the extent to which it is an *obstacle* to national state objectives, or an *agency* for national policy implementation, or an autonomous policy-maker, will vary greatly between national contexts. Local authorities may have a range of issues to decide upon that are totally irrelevant for sustainability policies, or they can, for example, have the political mandate to introduce long-term as well as short-term physical land-use plans, therefore going to the core of sustainability.

The shift from 'government towards governance' is especially evident in the local government context. A smaller scale of democratic decision-making seems to be quicker to respond to popular demands for changes in structures. And, arguably, it is a less risky business for the established national political elites to introduce institutional experiments and structural changes at the local government level. These changes can be introduced step by step, using pilot studies to 'test the water'.

Changes within local government focus on several different aspects: in the past, local government was often seen only as a bureaucratic organization, operating within well-established rules and patterns of behaviour. Such organizations are often 'closed' in the sense of being difficult for outsiders to penetrate or to influence. This pattern is under considerable pressure today. There are several ways through which local governments have become less 'closed', more 'open' and more receptive to external influences, especially interests at local level. Within a local context, local governments are also the agents best placed to respond (as opposed to other sectors of the community), since they possess the necessary resources and political legitimacy. Several studies show that the responsiveness of local governments is not only growing towards citizens, as a whole – 'activated participation'; more specialized groups are also being invited to have closer cooperation with the local communities. New public management is often used as a collective term describing all efforts in this direction. The groups considered in this respect are end-users of services and interest groups/organizations.

Therefore, sustainable development capacity-building efforts within the existing institutional structures, in our case local governments, can be defined as *all measures that strengthen the governmental structures to meet the demands of sustainable development, as well as measures that create these capacities in cooperation with civil society.*

The importance of the local government level is, however, often bypassed, either by local communities and civil society, or by national-level capacity-building efforts, in recent theoretical literature. For example, studies identifying different ecological modernization features have often neglected the local-level changes. Gibbs (2000) notes, however, that the theoretical construction of environmental policy capacity by Jänicke (1997) is, in fact, well suited to analyse local-level changes. Gibbs (2000) concludes in his study of regional-level ecological modernization in the UK that ecological modernization theory still has useful applications at the sub-national level.

LOCAL GOVERNMENT CAPACITY-BUILDING AS A STEP TOWARDS GOVERNANCE?

The emergence of a process of governance involves changes in at least two central characteristics of local government. This depends, of course, on the limitations that are imposed on local decision-making by national government.

First, changes occur in the institutional bases for local government. A change from static structures towards cooperative networks is evident in light of research by commentators such as Marsh and Rhodes (1992). To some extent, this development can be seen as a re-introduction of a corporatist tradition, but including new players, not just the traditional labour-market organizations. The introduction of these new actors – for instance, environmental organizations and professional experts – is of central importance in reaching consensus in difficult delimiting decisions that the new politics of sustainability bring along. The constitution of these new network-based policy-making communities differs from the traditional decision-making structures. Networks are highly flexible – in some matters the debate can be in the hands of a close policy community, in others discussible within a large issue network (Rhodes, 1996). It is also evident that the new structures are emerging on all societal levels. Recent research shows that the mode of governance is a central factor in relation to environmental conflicts in local communities. For example, Kettunen (1998) found that a higher degree of political and administrative openness in municipalities clearly limits the extent of local conflict.

Uhrwing (2001), however, provides a note of caution in her thesis entitled *Access to the Rooms of Power; Interest Organizations and Decision-making in Environmental Politics*. She notes that even if interest organizations (and, for that matter, individuals) are allowed into the decision-making forums, the possibilities of real input depend mostly upon the basic resources available. This is, according to her, also evident in Sweden, a society with long-term traditions of open access and transparency. It is a simple fact that intensive devotion and the voice (i.e. the possibility of being heard by different actors) is not enough in most cases.

The second visible change towards governance also means a broadened field of political participation. The changes in the democratic institutions from representative democracy towards a higher degree of direct and participative democracy are also clearly a feature that is at the core of processes of change. Local-level knowledge is thus important, especially when decisions should have an effect on local- and individual-level behaviour. Moreover, to neglect the wishes of the people for change might, in the long run, have a negative effect even on our basic democratic institutions (Joas, 2001).

It is evident that the capacity of a local government to develop cooperative patterns with the local civil society depends both on the type of problem to be solved and the historic pattern of policy-making and policy delivery within society. Furthermore, the new local-level institutions that are created might suffer from the collective action problem, as well as from an intensity problem – small but intensively active groups tend to steer non-political action (Rydin and Pennington, 2000). In general, however, earlier studies have indicated that the institution-building or capacity-building phase, steered by local government, seems to be one path to improving the opportunities of the public to participate, as well as to achieve successful policy outcomes for sustainable development. The creation of public spaces for debate without real influence on the political process is much less likely to work, according to Rydin and Pennington (2000).

The ways in which new institutional structures are created is, of course, a critical variable that explains differences in the degree of policy success. Empirical analyses have shown that 'in some cases, good governance can be achieved by decentralized and participatory approaches, but in other cases by centralized governance structure' (Roy and Tisdell, 1998, p1323). This empirical relationship is also noted by Pennington and Rydin (2000, p237) when they refer to the extensive work of Ellinor Ostrom (1990, 2000) and conclude that: 'there is surely a sufficiently wide body of research which confirms the importance of local capacity-building and participation in avoiding the policy failures that have often characterized more centralized planning schemes'.

CAPACITY-BUILDING FOR URBAN SUSTAINABLE DEVELOPMENT

This chapter seeks to draw together the distinct, yet linked, elements of capacity-building for urban sustainable development, and to explore how these processes interact at the interface of local government and civil society. The term 'capacity-building' has been applied, both in relation to policy-making at local level, in general, and specifically in terms of LA21 and other initiatives for sustainable development. For example, the United Nations Development Programme's (UNDP's) Capacity 21 programme understands capacity-building as 'the sum of the efforts needed to nurture, enhance and utilize the skills of people and institutions to progress towards sustainable development' (UNDP, 1999).

The concept of capacity-building has a particularly prominent place in contemporary environmental policy-making. It was identified as the principal *'means of implementation'* for most of the programme areas of the 1992 Rio Earth Summit Agenda 21 agreement, and as such it has become an important element in LA21 programmes worldwide. Capacity-building is usually understood as a *process that strengthens the ability of local communities and organizations to build their structures, systems, people and skills in order to undertake and develop initiatives that will contribute to sustainable development*, and during the last five to eight years there have been a number of European local capacity-building initiatives that are designed to develop local community capabilities for sustainable development.

The building of social capital and the development of community leadership may be viewed as the principal goals of capacity-building initiatives. Equally, the existence of effective community leaders is a central element in the development of social capital. Moreover, individuals within both civil society and local government have a key role to play in building capacity that can, in turn, contribute to what we call 'good governance' for sustainable development.

Supporting the development and maintenance of 'bridging social capital' could be through the mechanism of community leadership. Purdue (2001) notes that community leaders (both in local government and civil society) need to act as 'social entrepreneurs', building what he terms as 'communal social capital' (within their own organization) and 'collaborative social capital' (externally, in their relationship with other organizations). This perspective thus reinforces arguments about the pivotal role that community leaders have to play in processes of capacity-building for urban sustainable development.

Building up local knowledge and *building on* local knowledge seems to be the key to developing functional social capital and institutional capital. Healey (1998) comments on the importance of local knowledge within different sectors of civil society, and emphasizes that there is a need for local government to learn about *different social worlds*. This view is echoed by Taylor (2000), who argues that local communities do bring significant local knowledge to the table, and that this has been undervalued in the past. She suggests that little attention has been given by local government to building capacity in partner institutions, due to the assumption that the skills and knowledge deficit lies within local communities. This clearly links to wider debates on the 'shift' within local government from government to governance and the importance of greater interaction with civil society. For Healey, in order for local government to build assets in terms of social capital and *intellectual capital*, local policy-makers need to build up processes of social learning (that is, capacity-building).

Institutional capital (which for Healey, 1998, encompasses intellectual capital, social capital and political capital) should assist local government in responding flexibly to new circumstances and mobilizing resources. Within this framework, Healey emphasizes the existence of the repository of local *knowledge within civil society* as one reason for widening public involvement in policy development (that is, utilizing *expertise from 'outside'*), and learning about different 'social worlds' from which stakeholder groups and organizations come. Indeed, the LASALA project (Evans and Theobald, 2001) has identified the increasing involvement of 'experts' from outside local government as evidence of a shift towards local 'governance'. Healey suggests that the challenge for policy-making is thus to build up processes of social learning through which it becomes possible for a range of 'stakeholders' to collaborate in decision-making processes, and thus to avoid the time, cost and institutional damage of adversarial conflict resolution in these processes.

PARTNERSHIPS AND COOPERATION

Linked to debates on the relationship between local government and civil society is the discourse of *partnership* between agencies in the development and implementation of policies. Community involvement and partnership are hard to achieve, and there are tensions inherent in the notion and practice of community empowerment. The process of involving *multiple stakeholders* in decision-making 'raises tensions between the integrity that is required if local communities are to make a mark on partnership decisions and the diversity that needs to be respected if they are to have any legitimacy' (Taylor, 2000, p1028). The new ways of working and recasting power relationships that partnership implies will require a substantial learning programme to develop the essential new skills and capacities among professionals. Thus, the focus here is on the need for institutional capacity-building and institutional learning.

Purdue (2001) emphasizes the major power inequalities that persist between local authority and community representatives. Maloney et al (2000) provide a useful explanation of the uneven distribution of power between local government and other stakeholder groups. They employ the concept of the *political opportunity structure* in order to understand the ways in which this distribution of power impacts upon the ability of civil society organizations to engage with public authorities. The political opportunity structure has substantial influence on the uneven distribution of social capital as it affects:

> ...activities of civic associations and their ability to access and generate social capital. Where local authorities develop new partnerships, they are not only creating opportunities for developing new forms of relationships with other local actors, but will also affect previous social capital relationships with associations (Maloney et al, 2000, p817).

LOCAL POLITICS AND INSTITUTIONAL DESIGN

The work of Lowndes and Wilson (2001) explores the interface of local government capacity-building and social capital in a broad context. It addresses what the authors perceive as the growing critical response to Putnam's earlier work on social capital, in particular his neglect of the role of government. Putnam (1995) asserts that civic communities are self-reinforcing: civic engagement and good government become locked together in a 'virtuous circle'. He emphasizes that social capital is formed by and within civil society. He does, however, acknowledge in more recent work that social capital 'may also be strongly affected by the policy of governments and by the structure of government, itself a top-down process' (Putnam, 2000, p17).

Lowndes and Wilson (2001) argue that Putnam's perspective on social capital places insufficient importance on state agency. They emphasize the importance of local politics and the role of *institutional design* in explaining how governments can shape the development of social capital and its potential influence on democratic performance. Moreover, in their view, as well as influencing the creation of social capital, government seems likely to affect its mobilization. Thus, the underlying institutional framework of government is a crucial factor in determining the long-term prospects for social capital within civil society. Lowndes and Wilson (2001) propose four interacting dimensions of institutional design within local governance that shape the creation and mobilization of social capital:

1 *Relationships with the voluntary sector*: this is about local government support and recognition of voluntary associations, and whether there is an *instrumental* rather than a *democratic* approach to local authority/voluntary-sector relationships.
2 *Opportunities for citizen participation*: the institutional design of local *governance* may influence prospects for the formation of new groups and new stocks of social capital. Well-designed political institutions are crucial to fostering civic spirit as they provide the 'enabling' conditions for this to develop. However, local authorities may, in practice, rank service improvement as the main purpose of participation, ahead of citizen development and building social capital. This is, perhaps, not surprising since for many local authorities the provision of key statutory (and non-statutory) services is their main function.
3 *Responsiveness of decision-making*: even where there are institutional arrangements to involve citizens and groups in policy formulation, social capital can only have an impact on democratic processes where policy-makers actually take account of citizen's preferences. Even where high levels of social capital exist, government institutions may be structured in such a way that no 'benefit' from social capital accrues to formal democratic processes. The *demand* of social capital needs to match the *supply* for this within the political process.
4 *Democratic leadership and social inclusion*: public participation is a necessary but not a sufficient condition for democracy. Indeed, extending participation can mean more power for those already in advantaged positions. The relationship between social capital and democracy is therefore shaped by the capacity of governing institutions to listen to, and channel the range of, citizen demands.

Lowndes and Wilson (2001) note that 'good' institutional design does not always go alongside high levels of social capital. Indeed, 'bad' institutional design may have a positive impact on social capital – for example, through the mobilization of excluded groups over a particular issue.

DEFINING 'SUCCESS' IN URBAN SUSTAINABILITY

As the preceding discussion has indicated, there is a large body of both theoretical and empirical work on the independent variables in our research. We are thus guided by a common understanding of what is expected to be 'good' governance in relation to the society as a whole.

The problem with several of the definitions of successful sustainable development policy – such as the Aalborg Charter Principles or Agenda 21 – is that they include both procedural aspects of policies (different methods and tools to achieve certain goals), as well as indicators on progress within the relevant policy areas. To use a pre-existing listing of indicators of 'success' is therefore problematic because of the need to separate the independent variables (factors that are expected to have an effect on the policy outcomes themselves) and the dependent variable (policy outcomes themselves). However, if handled with caution, these will guide us towards an operational definition of sustainable development policy success.

The traditional way of measuring policy outcomes is to measure in terms of key indicators for sustainable development. However, as for the general goals, existing indicator systems include indicators that define policy and administrative procedures, as well as policy outcomes. For example, participation is just a means of achieving better policy results, not an indicator for sustainability as such.

Definitions of success in sustainability include the three pillars – environmental, social and economic progress – in such a way that achieving progress for one pillar should not harm the others. Our interest is not in defining a new concept of measurement for this task; instead, we rely on existing definitions of the topic. Of particular relevance here is an approach that follows the Aalborg Charter Principles (1994, revised in 1996 and 2000). This issue is further elaborated upon in Chapter 3.

THE THEORETICAL MODEL: EXPLAINING THE RELATIONSHIP BETWEEN CIVIL SOCIETY AND LOCAL GOVERNMENT IN THE SPHERE OF URBAN SUSTAINABLE DEVELOPMENT

As seen above, there is a strong relationship between institutional capital and social capital. At the local level (as at national level), this relationship is extremely complex, and the existence of a range of active organizations in civil society in any given locality does not necessarily mean that partnership between these and local government is effective. A key point in the debates on the nature of this relationship is that, as well as influencing the creation of social capital, government seems likely to affect its *mobilization*. Thus, the underlying institutional framework of government is a crucial factor in determining the long-term prospects for social capital within civil society.

Our basic assumption, based on the literature analysis above, is that *existing institutional structures and existing social capital within a society impact upon each other*. This interaction is a condition for all forms of democratic government, and even more in forms of governance where a society moves beyond the traditional mode of democratic rule. Furthermore, our assumption is that different forms of institutional structures lead to different levels of institutional capacities for sustainable policy-making. In a societal setting where (local) government capacities are generally at a high level, we could also expect that this would be the case in the sustainable development sector. A high degree of basic institutional capital provides a solid base for sustainable development capacity.

This capacity can be enhanced within existing structures – such as institutional capacity-building and institutional learning – and/or in cooperation with civil society. This capacity-building is mutually reinforcing in the sense that pre-existing institutions can be expected to enhance the possibilities of the civil society to take part in governance processes.

An assumption could also be made that a high level of social capital can be a basis for a high level of sustainable development capacity within civil society. Within civil society we can also find independent capacity-building measures, but we expect this activity to be less important. However, joint capacity-building measures with (local) government may lead to sustainable development policy success. Based on the assumptions in the current academic and policy discourses on 'good' governance and sustainable development policy processes, it is possible to establish the following proposition.

The higher the levels of both social and institutional capital, the greater the likelihood of sustainable development policy success. We call this *dynamic governing* for sustainable development (see Table 2.1).

Table 2.1 *Scenarios for different modes of governance and their impact on sustainable development (SD) policy outcome*

	Institutional capacity for sustainable development (SD)	
Social capacity for SD	*Higher*	*Lower*
Higher	1 Dynamic governing →High SD policy success	4 Voluntary governing →Low SD policy success
Lower	2 Active government →Medium SD policy success	3 Passive government →SD policy failure

Conversely, it could be argued that the lower the levels of social capital and institutional capital, the greater the likelihood of sustainable development policy failure. *Passive government* may reach policy outcome based on routine operations or residual effects of governance from other societal levels.

In our second scenario the assumption is that better results can be achieved if the institutional structures, at least – that is, local governments – have clearly included the goals of sustainability within their activities. This kind of *active government* can, from a theoretical point of view, be *(eco-)efficient* as a mode of governing – at least regarding some sustainable development policies that are less sensitive to the need for public participation.

A more problematic case – *voluntary governing* – is the situation where civil society is expected to act almost alone in order to reach sustainability. To rely just on a high social capacity for sustainable development could present rather limited possibilities to achieve sustainable development policy success.

Our next step is to take the model further from theory to reality. How do we make our concepts operational and measurable? A central problem while making the model measurable is that it is never an easy task to measure abstract concepts such as policy success or governance. Nevertheless, we have to provide the mechanisms to do this, and we discuss this in further detail in Appendix A on the methodological framework. Each empirical chapter will also present the data that is utilized in the analysis.

Drawing upon the research data from our 40 towns and cities, the following chapters examine, in turn, the areas of policy achievement (Chapter 3), the character of institutional and social capacity (Chapter 4), and the ways in which local governments interact with their civil societies (Chapter 5). These chapters then form the basis for the conclusions contained in Chapter 6 and the recommendations for action that comprise Chapter 7.

Meeting the Sustainability Challenge

INTRODUCTION

This is the first of two empirical chapters, which present the data on the dependent variable in our research: sustainable development policy 'success'. As noted in Chapter 2, the Aalborg Charter Principles provide a useful starting point from which to examine the progress of European towns and cities towards policy 'success' in this area. The Principles include a number of broad indicators of 'success': the maintenance and preservation of natural capital; sustainable land-use patterns; sustainable urban mobility patterns; responsibility for the global climate; and the social needs of citizens. All of these aspects were considered in developing the methodology, and particularly in the questions posed both in the interviews and questionnaires.

We felt that in the analysis and presentation of the findings on 'success' it was more appropriate to think in terms of 'progress' with sustainable development or sustainability 'policy outcomes' since 'success' is relative, and varied greatly according to the city, country or 'region' of Europe that we studied. Instead, we focus on the 'policy outcomes' – in terms of explicit policies and actions within each case study, as perceived by the local government and civil society respondents, and also in the judgement of the fieldworkers. In this, and the subsequent empirical chapters *local government* refers to the local level of governing in general; *local authority* is used for the specific case studies, and encompasses both the administration and political aspects; and *municipality* refers to the geographical area for which the local authority is responsible.

The material for this chapter is derived from four sources: interviews, document analysis, questionnaires and fieldworker summary reports. The interviews are used to show the range of topics being addressed in all of the 40 towns and cities (referred to as 'case studies'). The questionnaire responses are compared with the interview findings for the top 20 case studies (described later on in the chapter) in order to identify the main areas where local government and civil society respondents concur in their opinions. These sources of data are combined with document analysis and the fieldworker summary reports to provide evidence of *tangible policy outcomes*. However, we recognize that in some cases the responses do not tally with what is happening in reality (for example, when examining the documents and the fieldworkers' information on concrete actions that have taken place), and this is noted where relevant. The material thus builds up a 'picture' of the extent and areas of progress across the 40 case studies (see Box 3.1). It then identifies the top five case studies from each of the four regions and discusses these in further detail.

Box 3.1 *The 40 case studies*

Northern Europe

1 Frederikshavn, Denmark
2 Albertslund, Denmark
3 Gotland, Sweden
4 Falkenberg, Sweden
5 Växjö, Sweden
6 Lahti, Finland
7 Stavanger, Norway
8 South-west Finland Agenda, Finland
9 Tampere, Finland
10 Vantaa, Finland

Eastern Europe

1 Tallinn City, Estonia
2 Kuressaare, Estonia
3 Korolev, Russia
4 Anyksciai, Lithuania
5 Dunajska Luzna, Slovakia
6 Gdansk, Poland
7 Veliko Turnovo, Bulgaria
8 Orastie, Romania
9 Baia Mare, Romania
10 Dubrovnik, Croatia

Western Europe

1 Durham County Council, UK
2 London Borough of Redbridge, UK
3 Stirling, UK
4 Dungannon and South Tyrone, Northern Ireland, UK
5 Ottignies-Louvain la Neuve, Belgium
6 Haarlem, The Netherlands
7 Munich, Germany
8 Hanover, Germany
9 Valenciennes, France
10 Dunkerque Urban Community, France

Southern Europe

1 Calvià, Spain
2 Granollers, Spain
3 Santa Perpetua de Mogoda, Spain
4 Barcelona Province, Spain
5 Celle Ligure, Italy
6 Modena Province, Italy
7 Fano, Italy
8 Ferrara, Italy
9 Thessaloniki, Greece
10 Beja, Portugal

In the discussion of the findings, not all of the initiatives and actions that occur across the 40 case studies are presented – indeed, this was not the primary aim of the research. Rather, what emerges are the perceptions and knowledge of the interviewees and questionnaire respondents on the sustainability issues that their local authorities are addressing. From these we have been able to distinguish between different types of activities – namely, those that:

- take place because of national government requirements, such as recycling targets;
- are supported and/or funded at national or regional level, but which local authorities can voluntarily 'sign up' to – for instance, the Green Flag project

in Northern European countries; 'eco-municipalities' in Sweden; the Local Agenda 21 (LA21) model in Barcelona, Spain; and the LA21 network for the South-west Finland Agenda;
- local authorities themselves initiate, without financial assistance or guidance from regional or national level.

AREAS OF PROGRESS IN THE 40 CASE STUDIES

Table 3.1 sets out a selection of the environmental, social, and economic topics that have been mentioned in the interviews with local government and civil society organizations, and indicates some of the towns and cities where these topics are explicitly cited. The majority of the responses cite environmental protection as the area where most progress has been made, and this is reflected in the range of topics described below, contrasting with the smaller number of examples of social and economic sustainability.

As Table 3.1 shows, actions for energy efficiency and the promotion of renewable energy are occurring in a number of the case studies. In some instances this forms part of a wider policy approach to climate protection (for example, in the case of those towns and cities becoming members of the Climate Alliance and its Nordic equivalent: KLIMP). One notable cross-national initiative is the Green Flag project operating in the Northern European countries, and which focuses on the development of renewable energy sources in schools and day-care centres. Several of the case studies, again mainly in the Northern European region, have been developing renewable energy policies in terms of wind power plants, solar power and biogas.

In the area of transport and mobility, respondents in the majority of the 40 cases perceive that their local authorities have made some progress in this area, particularly in relation to projects for improving cyclist and pedestrian routes and zones. Such actions would not necessarily be described as innovative; however, they are clearly relevant as examples of environmental improvements and are visible to the public. Several cases report progress in the provision of less-polluting public transport vehicles, and in the two German cases there were examples of projects on car sharing, and subsidizing public transport. A high proportion of interviewees across all of the case studies cited the reliance on travelling by car, and therefore the difficulty of trying to convince individuals to use other forms of transport as a major obstacle to progressing in this area.

In the area of nature protection, a number of the case studies are either protecting or extending green spaces and establishing biodiversity policies. This tends to be local authority led; however, one interesting example is that of cooperation by the local authority with environmental non-governmental organizations (NGOs) on a nature school, funded for five years by the local authority (Vantaa, Finland).

For several of the Eastern European case studies, the main areas of progress are perceived as waste management, improving wastewater collection and cleaning up beaches. In some of these examples, the promotion of the municipality

Table 3.1 *Environmental topics*

Climate protection	• Member of Climate Alliance/KLIMP (*Munich; Hanover; Gotland; Stavanger*) • Setting up Climate Protection Agency and Fund (*Hanover*) • 'Fossil fuel-free' city (*Växjö*)
Energy efficiency	• Eco-improvements for housing (*Hanover*) • Model projects for energy efficiency (*Munich*) • Energy-saving initiatives (*Vantaa; Korolev; Tampere; Albertslund; Stavanger*) • Improving heating systems in public buildings (*Modena Province; Dungannon and South Tyrone*)
Renewable energy	• Renewables policies, e.g. wind power (*Frederikshavn; Falkenberg; Gotland; Tampere*) • Model projects for solar energy (*London Borough of Redbridge; Beja*) • Methane gas plant (*Ferrara*) • Biogas project (*Falkenberg*)
Transport	• Cooperation between local authority and car-sharing agency (*Hanover*) • Schemes for subsidizing public transport for local government employees and for improving rail and bus services (*Hanover*) • Less-polluting buses (*Gotland; Dunkerque Urban Community*) • Eco-Sundays (car-free areas in city) (*Fano; Celle Ligure*) • Electric cars used by local government employees (*Dunkerque Urban Community*) • Cycle path/route construction (*Falkenberg; Munich; Gdansk; Anyksciai; Ferrara; Calvià; Santa Perpetua de Mogoda*) • Pedestrian areas/zones (*Beja; Falkenberg; Santa Perpetua de Mogoda; Calvià; Ferrara*)
Nature protection	• Cooperation between local authority and industry on creating green spaces (*Haarlem*) • Protection of rare plants and nature areas (*Anyksciai; Beja; South-west Finland Agenda*) • Local authority ceasing use of pesticides (*Albertslund*) • Pilot local authority for National Association for Nature Protection (*Växjö*) • Buying up land for nature reserves (*Vantaa*) • Nature school funded by local authority (*Vantaa*)
Water management	• Improving wastewater collection (*Dubrovnik; Gdansk; Calvià*) • Cleaner beaches/coastline (*Dubrovnik; Gdansk; Calvià; Durham County Council*) • Reduction in water usage (*Calvià*)

Table 3.1 *(continued)*

Waste management	• Creation of recycling facilities/initiatives (*Veliko Turnovo; Gdansk; Dunajska Luzna; Dungannon and South Tyrone; Tampere; Frederikshavn*) • Municipal composting initiatives (*Santa Perpetua de Mogoda; Frederikshavn*)
Improving practices in local government and its institutions	• Renewable energy in schools and day-care centres through Green Flag Project (*Frederikshavn; South-west Finland Agenda; Gotland; Stavanger*) • 'Eco-food' in schools and local authority (*Albertslund*) • Wood certification scheme (*Valenciennes*) • Improving recycling in local authority (*Santa Perpetua de Mogoda*) • Purchasing policy favouring high environmental requirements (*Stavanger; Barcelona Province*)
Environmental policy tools	• Environmental Management and Audit Scheme (EMAS) (*Albertslund*) • Environmental audit programme (*Barcelona Province*) • Eco-budget (*Ferrara, Växjö*) • Eco-profit (*Hanover*) • Eco-audit (*Hanover*) • Ecological footprinting (*Vantaa*) • Precautionary principle used in decision-making (*Dunajska Luzna*) • LA21 (for example in *Gdansk; Baia Mare; Gotland; Albertslund; Stavanger; Santa Perpetua de Mogoda; Barcelona Province; Ferrara; Modena Province*)

as an attractive place for tourism, or for business to locate and invest in, also means a strong emphasis on attracting inward investment – particularly from the European Union (EU) – in order to improve infrastructure such as roads, educational facilities and public health buildings. Waste and water issues are addressed in a more explicit 'sustainable tourism' framework in Calvià (Spain) in terms of decreasing waste, improving recycling and reducing water usage.

The interviews highlight a number of examples of good practice being developed by local authorities for their own institutions. In Albertslund (Denmark) 'eco-food' is provided in 95 per cent of local authority institutions (schools and day-care centres), and this initiative is linked to the cross-national Green Flag project. Other examples include that of Santa Perpetua de Mogoda (Spain), which is involved in developing 'good housekeeping' for waste within the local authority in terms of improving recycling and developing a composting network in the municipality. Many local authorities are also adopting environmental policy tools as part of their sustainability strategy. Policy tools cited in the interviews are eco-procurement; eco-budget; ecological footprinting;

LA21; environmental audit; eco-profit; Environmental Management and Audit Scheme (EMAS); and International Standards Organization (ISO) environmental standard ISO14001. In many of the case studies LA21 is perceived as both active and influential in progressing with sustainable development policy implementation. What is apparent from the comments on environmental policy tools is that these can clearly be seen as part of the 'story' of progress, as well as part of the process in terms of the 'value added' in sustainable development policy implementation.

SOCIAL EQUITY TOPICS

As shown in Table 3.2, a small number of social equity issues are mentioned in the interviews, and this clearly reflects a smaller emphasis on these issues in all of the 40 case studies, compared to the environmental dimensions of sustainability. Mobility aspects are also mentioned under this heading, as these particular examples refer explicitly to assisting particular social groups, rather than to mobility policies, in general.

Table 3.2 *Social equity topics*

Mobility	• Financial assistance for travel for some social groups (*Ottignies-Louvain la Neuve*) • Social taxi initiative (*Dunajska Luzna*)
Education	• Building new higher education institutions and libraries (*Beja; Korolev*)
Services for vulnerable groups	• Building recreational facilities for young people (*Veliko Turnovo*) • Social cooperation with groups for the elderly and disabled (*Calvià; Celle Ligure*) • 'My-bus' initiative for elderly residents (*Fano*) • Italian lessons for ethnic minority groups (*Fano*)
Employment	• Local Employment Agency for sustainable development jobs (*Dunkerque Urban Community; Calvià*) • Job creation through EXPO initiative (*Hanover*)

These topic areas range from building or developing public institutions (for example, higher education institutions and public libraries) to the 'My-bus' initiative in Fano (Italy), designed for elderly people, and to initiatives such as free Italian lessons for ethnic minority groups. In addition, some interesting areas are developing in the social arena, which are explicitly making links to environmental and economic aspects. For instance, in Ottignies-Louvain la

Neuve (Belgium) there is reference to the Mobility Plan and projects emanating from this which focus on assisting with mobility for excluded groups. Both Calvià and Dunkerque Urban Community (France) have established a local employment agency for sustainable development work.

SUSTAINABLE ECONOMY TOPICS

Table 3.3 presents some examples of sustainable economy projects and initiatives cited in the interviews.

Table 3.3 *Sustainable economy topics*

Working with business and industry	• Working with business and public utilities on climate energy initiatives (*South-west Finland Agenda*) • Working with business on recycling projects (*Dubrovnik*) • Promotion of environmental practices in business and industry (*Durham County Council*) • Working with business on sustainable tourism (*Calvià*) • Creating an environmentally friendly company as a model (*Lahti*) • Eco-profit initiative for farmers and for small- and medium-sized enterprises (SMEs) (*Falkenberg; Hanover*) • Cooperation with car industry (*Munich*)
Regulating business/industry	• Tightening development regulations (*Tallinn*) • Environmental public inspectorate (*Veliko Turnovo*) • Environmental industrial plan (*Dunkerque Urban Community*) • Strengthening environmental regulations for construction (*Tallinn*)
Local economy	• Promoting use of local products (*Falkenberg*)
Global economy	• Promoting and using fair trade products (*Munich; Hanover; Dunkerque Urban Community; Valenciennes*)
Taxation	• Eco-tax for holiday-makers (*Calvià*)

As the examples in Table 3.3 show, there is evidence of local authorities linking with business in environmental projects, and also of promoting environmental practices in business and industry – for instance, through the encouragement of small- and medium-sized enterprises (SMEs) to adopt EMAS. There is a number of examples of local authorities promoting development and activities in the economic arena, particularly through an eco-profit scheme (Falkenberg and Hanover), the promotion of local products (Falkenberg) and fair trade activities (Hanover, Munich, Valenciennes, Dunkerque Urban Community). One particularly innovative example is of Hanover creating its own brand of fair trade coffee.

Box 3.2 illustrates a selection of the examples of environmental, social and economic progress outlined in the discussion so far in order to show the range of more 'innovative' projects being undertaken.

Box 3.2 *'Innovative' examples of sustainability progress*

ENVIRONMENTAL ASPECTS

Hanover

Through Hanover's 'Job-ticket' scheme, there is subsidized public transport for commuting employees and improvements to the light- and heavy-rail networks. Bus lanes have also been subsidized by the city.

Hanover has set up a Climate Protection Fund – ProKlima – with the city utility and five neighbouring local authorities. It has also set up the Climate Protection Agency with other local authorities, the local public transport operator, and the utility and private companies, which coordinates all climate protection activities in the region.

Gotland, Albertslund, Frederikshavn, South-west Finland Agenda

These feature the Green Flag project (for developing renewable energy in schools and day-care centres).

Dunkerque Urban Community

Here, buses run on gas and employees use electric cars.

Albertslund

'Eco-food' is eaten in 95 per cent of local authority institutions (schools and day-care centres).

Växjö

In Växjö a fossil fuel-free initiative, with the aim of reducing fossil fuel emissions by 50 per cent by 2010, involves cooperation between the local authority, university and private sector.

Ferrara

Here, a methane plant was built to increase the level of renewable energy for the city.

Vantaa

In cooperation with environmental NGOs, the local authority set up and funded (for a period of five years) a nature school.

Albertslund

The municipality of Albertslund ceased its use of pesticides.

Box 3.2 *(continued)*

SOCIAL EQUITY ASPECTS

Dunajska Luzna

Here, a social taxi is run by civil society volunteers.

Calvià

Calvià features a local employment agency for sustainable development jobs – IFOC – and a 'social cooperation' initiative with elderly and disabled people.

Dunkerque Urban Community

Here, a local employment agency for sustainable development work in waste management operates.

ECONOMIC ASPECTS

Tallinn

Tallinn removed a clause in development plans in order to tighten up on developments that do not abide by environmental regulations.

Lahti

Lahti started an environmentally friendly company in 1996 as a good model for other companies to use.

Hanover

Hanover features its fair-traded organically grown coffee.

Calvià

Calvià works in partnership with hotels to develop sustainable tourism and the promotion of the eco-tax for both residents and tourists.

TOP 20 CASE STUDIES IN THE RESEARCH

Following on from the presentation of the topic areas across the 40 case studies, the next step was to make a judgement of where progress was most evident. To do this, a scoring device was used in order to rank the extent of progress (or 'policy outcomes'). All case studies were given a ranking between *low extent* to *high extent. Low extent* was then given a score of 5, *medium extent* a score of 10 and *high extent* a score of 15, although where it was judged that cases fell between these, a mid-way score was allocated (for example, *low-medium* is 7.5). Case studies were scored within their region (each of the four 'regions' contained ten cases) in order to identify the 'top case studies' (the total was five from each region). Perhaps not surprisingly, the scorings are generally highest in the Northern European case studies and lowest in the Eastern European case studies, and this reflects the findings that progress for sustainable development is more advanced in the former region. Many of the new member states in the EU (some of those in the Eastern European category) have only recently been addressing environmental protection issues or, more broadly, sustainable development. Thus, a city in Sweden may have scored higher than one in Poland, but is still not in the top five of its 'region'. This does not imply that it has achieved less, but that the score was lower in the context of the 'region' only. Of the 20 case studies selected, 18 are in the category of 'good practice for sustainable development' (Sustainable Cities and Towns Award Winners or Local Authorities' Self-Assessment of Local Agenda – LASALA – Good Practice), and only two are in the 'reference' group – those which were not known to have an explicit sustainable development or LA21 strategy at the time of selection. Table 3.4 shows the top five case studies in each of the regions based on the scoring system explained above.

For each of the 20 case studies in Table 3.4, a brief description is given below of their context. The relevant documents examined by the fieldworkers are noted (except for those cases where the documents were not available or could not be collected). Second, the key areas of progress from the interviews

Table 3.4 *Top 20 case studies for policy outcomes*

City	Policy outcomes
Eastern European case studies	
Gdansk, Poland	10
Veliko Turnovo, Bulgaria	7.5
Korolev, Russia	5
Dunajska Luzna, Slovakia	5
Kuressaare, Estonia	5
Western European case studies	
Hanover, Germany	15
Munich, Germany	15
Dunkerque Urban Community, France	12.5
Ottignies-Louvain La Neuve, Belgium	7.5
Haarlem, The Netherlands	7.5
Southern European case studies	
Calvià, Spain	15
Ferrara, Italy	12.5
Barcelona Province, Spain	10
Modena Province, Italy	10
Santa Perpetua de Mogoda, Spain	7.5
Northern European case studies	
Gotland, Sweden	15
Albertslund, Denmark	12.5
Stavanger, Norway	10
Växjö, Sweden	10
Tampere, Finland	7.5

are provided, with some indication of the level of agreement between the local government and civil society respondents on the areas of progress.

The relevant questionnaire data are then presented in order to provide further evidence (or to note where these data contradict the interview findings) on the areas and level of progress as perceived by respondents. The questionnaire data cover the aspects of land-use planning and protection of green spaces; travel and mobility; climate protection; promotion of sustainability practices and partnerships with business and industry; social equity (poverty and unemployment measures, and affordable housing); and policy tools for sustainable development. For most of the questions respondents were given a choice of four options on a scale between 'no extent' and 'very high extent', the two middle ranges being 'a little extent' and 'high extent'. The responses in the 'high' and 'very high' extent categories are given as a combined percentage in order to provide an indication of the policy outcomes in the different areas. This is supplemented by considering the mean or 'average' of the responses for environmental, economic and social aspects for each case study (calculated by allocating a score of 0 to 3 to represent the range of 'extents' with 0 being 'no extent', and 3 being 'very high extent') (see Table 3.5). The aim is, therefore, to

Table 3.5 *'Averages' for environmental, economic and social sum indexes in the top 20 case studies*

Case study	Local government/civil society combined responses		
	Environment	Economic	Social
Korolev, Russia	1.9	2.4	2.5
Dunajska Luzna, Slovakia	1.9	2.5	2.6
Gdansk, Poland	2.6	2.3	2.4
Kuressaare, Estonia	2.1	2.4	2.1
Veliko Turnovo, Bulgaria	1.9	2.3	2.1
Hanover, Germany	3.0	2.4	3.1
Munich, Germany	2.8	2.5	2.5
Dunkerque Urban Community, France	2.4	2.5	2.8
Ottignies-Louvain la Neuve, Belgium	2.7	2.4	2.3
Haarlem, The Netherlands	2.2	2.4	2.3
Ferrara, Italy	2.6	2.6	2.5
Modena Province, Italy	2.5	2.8	2.2
Barcelona Province, Spain	2.3	1.9	2.1
Santa Perpetua de Mogoda, Spain	2.6	2.8	2.4
Calvià, Spain	2.3	2.8	2.3
Gotland, Sweden	2.6	2.5	2.4
Stavanger, Norway	2.5	2.5	2.4
Albertslund, Denmark	2.5	2.8	2.3
Tampere, Finland	2.4	2.2	2.2
Växjö, Sweden	2.9	2.6	2.6

build up a 'picture' of progress in the case studies from the opinions of all the respondents and from the different sources of data.

Top five case studies in Eastern Europe

Korolev, Russia (LASALA Good Practice)

Korolev has a population of 170,000. It is situated close to Moscow and has national support and funding for being a 'city of science' and a centre of space industry. Related to this, there is a focus on technology, in general, but also more specifically on investment in resource-saving technology. Three specific documents were seen to be relevant: The *Concept of Korolev Sustainable Development: Strategy of the City Transition towards Sustainable Development*; *Municipal Objective Programme for Saving Resources*; and *Ensuring Environmental Safety in Korolev. Main Directives of Korolev's City Development in the Field of the Environment until 2006* (Korolev City Administration 2000a, b, 2003). The first seems to indicate a high level of integration of the three sustainable development dimensions, but there is no time scale for action. The second has a number of measures on energy efficiency, although no specific examples of the latter were given in the interviews. The third sets out a number of measures for improving quality of life.

One notable social aspect mentioned in the interviews concerns the development of higher education institutions (in several of the interviews a highly educated population was perceived as central to achieving sustainability). The responses from both civil society and local government are broadly in agreement. The key issues are seen as the importance of visual changes in the city, the need for an educated population, and the need for creating and improving educational institutions.

The questionnaire data that correspond broadly to the social aspects show that 60 per cent of respondents think the local authority is addressing social equity issues to a high extent within its policies and strategies. The sum indexes show a lower 'average' for the environmental questions (1.9), but are higher for economic and social outcomes (2.4 and 2.5, respectively), which particularly reflects the emphasis in the interview responses on the social dimensions.

Dunajska Luzna, Slovakia (LASALA Good Practice)

Dunajska Luzna has a population of 3000 and is the smallest in population size of all the 40 case studies. It is fairly near to the capital, Bratislava, and therefore has a particular problem with young people migrating to work in the capital.

Sustainable development is perceived as environmental protection, and this is reflected in the relevant documents. The *Environmental Action Plan* includes actions on waste and ecological aspects. The second key document is the *Territorial Development Plan*, produced in 1996, which states a number of actions, although these have not been implemented. The third document is the *Sustainable Development Strategy*, which does not state specific actions, but does consider the interrelationship of the three dimensions of sustainability (Dunajska Luzna Local Authority (2000a, b, 2002).

A number of actions are cited in the interviews, and these are predominantly environmental, although there is also one example of social sustainability. The main areas are waste separation in elementary schools, the application of the precautionary principle when making decisions about new investments, and a social taxi run by a civil society organization. The interview responses from both civil society and local government do suggest close links between these, and it is possible that this relates to the population size. In particular, the LA21 forum is mentioned as being active and situated within the Community Environmental Association. The fieldworker report suggested that this organization is 'the driving force in Dunajska Luzna with regard to sustainable development, planning and education'.

The questionnaire data in relation to social equity shows that 80 per cent respond that the local authority has used its powers to a high extent to reduce poverty and unemployment, and 92 per cent say the local authority is addressing social equity issues to a high or very high extent in its policies. The sum indexes for environmental progress show the same 'average' as for Korolev – 1.9 – possibly reflecting a limited amount of progress on the environmental aspects. However, the social and economic 'averages' are much higher, both 2.6, which does seem to reflect the interviewee opinions on progress in the social aspects, in particular.

Gdansk, Poland (LASALA Good Practice)

Gdansk has a population of 400,000. According to the fieldworker report, it has major problems to address, including development of infrastructure for water, waste and transport, and also unemployment. Its approach to sustainable development has been through the environmental route, with the process starting in 1991. The focus has been to encourage tourism; but it has been recognized that without solving environmental problems (transport, water treatment, air pollution, waste management, nature protection), it is not possible to develop tourism effectively.

The principal relevant document is the *Development Strategy*, with a chapter on sustainable development principles (Gdansk City Administration, 1998). As part of this strategy, one of the operational programmes focuses on environmental protection, and this has been informed and developed by the LA21 forum – in particular, using the expertise of the organizations represented on the forum.

Reflecting the emphasis on tourism, the key issues mentioned in the interviews are cleaner beaches/water management, air pollution monitoring, improvement of cycling facilities and city restoration. However, there is a concern about increasing car usage in the city. Both local government and civil society interview respondents noted that there had been progress, although the latter felt that these were fairly minor 'successes', such as cycle paths. The relevant questionnaire data is on the provision of cycling facilities and this shows a high proportion – 78 per cent – perceiving this as happening to a high or very high extent. The sum indexes for all three dimensions of sustainable development are fairly high – the average for the environment questions is 2.6, 2.3 for the economic questions, and 2.4 for the social equity questions. This seems to reflect the fact that Gdansk is clearly addressing a number of areas that relate to the different aspects of sustainability, particularly in relation to developing the tourism sector.

Kuressaare, Estonia (LASALA Good Practice)

Kuressaare is a town in the county of Estonia and is situated on the island of Saaremaa. The population of Kuressaare is 16,000, and the 'city' is known as a city of resorts and health restoration, and as a holiday destination in the summer season. Tourism is one of the most important areas of revenue, and one of its aims is to link a healthy environment with sustainable development.

The two most relevant documents are the *General Plan* and the *Health and Sustainable Development Strategy* (Kuressaare City Government, 2000, 2001). The former covers housing, recreation facilities, infrastructure aspects such as sewage and water supply, and tourism. Also mentioned is the compilation of an energy-saving plan, and the target of 30 to 40 per cent of waste to be recycled by the year 2005.

From the interviews, it is noted that Kuressaare is a member of the Healthy Cities network. The main areas of progress cited are the reduction of water usage, the shifting of industry away from the city centre, and the use of wood chips for heating (moving away from the use of oil). The main area of contention in the interviews was between a representative of an environmental NGO and other respondents. The NGO representative suggested that the sustainable development plan is a 'façade' and that business ideas still dominate – for instance, in the planning process. The most relevant questionnaire data is on the local authority working in partnership with business and industry in addressing the environmental, social and economic issues in the municipality, to which 38 per cent respond that this is occurring to a high extent, but none to a very high extent. The sum index 'averages' are fairly high for all three sustainability aspects, at 2.1 for environmental outcomes, 2.4 for economic aspects and 2.1 for social outcomes.

Veliko Turnovo, Bulgaria (European Sustainable Cities and Towns Award Winner 1997)

Veliko Turnovo is a very old city with a population of approximately 100,000. Being small in relation to other cities in Bulgaria, it lacks the pressures faced by some bigger cities. City life is situated around the centre and the main street, and the city has a fairly young population due to the existence of the local university.

The key documents are the *Strategy for Development* and the *Strategy for Sustainable Development* (Veliko Turnovo City Council, 2000a, b). The main objectives of the former are to create conditions for sustainable and balanced development of the city, to get involved in national, European and international projects, and to improve quality of life for citizens. The *Strategy for Sustainable Development* tends to focus more on the economic dimensions of sustainability, but in terms of economic growth and inward investment in the city, rather than on linking economy with environment and social issues. The interviews cite the main areas of progress as waste and river management, and the creation of an environmental public inspectorate. One of the civil society respondents comments that the city is, 'by chance', a very clean place, so there are no major environmental problems to deal with. There have also been cultural events, such as an Earth Day and a folklore festival. Tourism seems to be seen as having a positive influence in terms of sustainability, and accession funds have been perceived as assisting with progress. One example of action in the social arena is the development of recreational facilities for young people. Both local government and civil society respondents concur on some aspects of progress, although the conditions, as noted above, are favourable for achieving more environmental sustainability.

In the questionnaire, 40 per cent of individuals responded that the local authority is promoting environmentally beneficial practices in business and industry to a high extent, but fewer (29 per cent) responded that social equity issues are being addressed in policies and actions. The 'average' for the sum index on environmental questions is the same as for two of the other case studies in the 'region' (1.9); however, for social and economic outcomes the average is higher (2.1 and 2.3, respectively).

TOP FIVE CASE STUDIES IN WESTERN EUROPE

Hanover, Germany (LASALA Good Practice)

Hanover has a population of 0.5 million. It is a modern city, and, with over half of its area comprising green and open spaces, including a large forest inside the city, Hanover markets itself as a 'city of gardens'. The main issues for the city are perceived by respondents to be immigration and urban sprawl. The EXPO 2000 in the city is generally seen as being a boost economically, with the development of roads, public transport and train connections; however, the perception was that the longer-term benefits had not been as substantial as predicted.

According to the relevant documents for Hanover, sustainable development is a cross-cutting issue. The Climate Protection Programme has a central aim of reducing carbon dioxide emissions by 2005 and sets out clear actions for achieving this. The main areas of sustainable development progress for Hanover, according to the interviews, are transport and mobility, climate protection, and eco-procurement.

In the area of transport, it is noted that the city council and the Greater Hanover Authority together subsidize the public transport system. Through the 'Job-ticket' scheme, there is subsidized public transport for commuting employees, and improvements to the light- and heavy-rail networks and bus lanes have been subsidized by the city. There are policies to inhibit private car use and to encourage cycling and walking. A *FrauenNachtTaxi* service operates to bring women home from their tram or bus stop at night-time. A more recent initiative is cooperation between the publicly owned transport company and a car-sharing agency.

In terms of climate protection policies and initiatives for renewable energy, the local authority is a member of the Climate Alliance. It has developed a range of innovative approaches in this area. For example, it has set up a Climate Protection Fund, ProKlima, with the city utility and five neighbouring local authorities. ProKlima is a grant agency, which finances energy-optimization activities, and campaigns for carbon dioxide savings and the use of renewable energy. Hanover has also developed model projects to promote energy efficiency and renewable forms of energy, such as eco-improvements for housing. The local authority has set up the Climate Protection Agency with other local authorities, the local public transport operator, and the utility and private companies, and this agency coordinates all climate protection activities in the region.

The comments from both local government and civil society respondents in the interviews suggest a high level of agreement on the main areas of progress for Hanover: model projects; the setting up of an environment centre; climate protection work; and energy efficiency projects. It is also noted by the civil society sectors that public transport is very efficient. However, according to one of the civil society organizations, its success 'depends on the mentality of people: the offer of public transport is very good – now it is the people who have to decide how much they want to use the private car'.

From the questionnaire responses, 91 per cent responded that the local authority addresses climate change concerns in its policies and strategies to a high or very high extent, and 62 per cent that the local authority has been successful in reducing greenhouse gas emissions.

On transport issues, 67 per cent said the local authority is acting to a high or very high extent to reduce the need to travel; 91 per cent suggested that the local authority is improving public transport to a high or very high extent; and 100 per cent cited the provision of pedestrian and cycling facilities. The figures for climate protection and transport policies clearly reflect the responses in the interviews. In terms of policy tools, LA21 and eco-audit are cited in the interviews. However, one local government respondent noted that the existence of LA21 had not necessarily led to better results in Hanover.

On social issues, the interviews mention mobility planning as relating to the social aspects. A number of examples of sustainable economy initiatives are noted in the interviews, such as the eco-profit scheme for SMEs and the creation of a fairly traded organically grown Hanover coffee. The questionnaire responses in this area do not, however, reflect the high profile that interview respondents give to economic sustainability aspects. In relation to partnerships with business and industry in addressing sustainability issues, 52 per cent responded that this occurs to a high extent, while only 19 per cent believed that the local authority promotes environmentally and socially beneficial practices in business and industry. For the sum index for environmental outcomes, the 'average' is the highest of the five 'region' case studies, at 3, and also highest for social equity questions (3.1), with a lower (though still relatively high) average for economic issues (2.4). These reflect the progress being made across all three dimensions of sustainability, although the social and environmental aspects predominate.

Munich, Germany (European Sustainable Cities and Towns Award Winner 1999)

Munich has a population of 1.3 million, and the perspective from the fieldworker was that it is an attractive place in which to live and work. The city won the European Sustainable Cities and Towns Award in 1999. The main issues for Munich are dealing with traffic, housing and the redevelopment of brown-field sites.

The key documents that seem to be influencing the implementation of sustainable development are the *Urban Development Strategy* (UDS), and the *Council Goals* (City of Munich, 2002, 2003). The UDS is a legally binding plan for the city (it is prioritized above land-use planning), and this has been adopted despite not being mandatory in Germany. A number of model projects are cited within this plan to illustrate its key objectives, and these take into account the sustainability aspects. In turn, these objectives are binding for all of the city directorates. The *Council Goals* have sustainable development as a guide for political decisions and daily operations. These goals are also intended to complement the objectives in the UDS.

The interview responses indicate a number of areas of progress in all three dimensions of sustainability. The main areas are climate protection (Munich, like Hanover, is a member of the Climate Alliance); renewable energy; model projects on car-sharing and on solar energy; improvement of cycling facilities and routes; and cooperation between the car industry and local authority. The local authority also has a fair trade policy and actions that emanate from this. It has developed a Green City Initiative to promote many of these aspects; this could be perceived as both an area of progress and a capacity-building issue.

Both the local government and civil society sectors seem to agree on progress in mobility and model projects; but both note the limitations of projects in terms of their wider application. One local government respondent suggests that Munich is 'taking steps' to sustainable development, but actions need to be more widespread. There are also concerns about the car industry lobby acting against the city's policies to reduce car use, and also about the expensive land prices in the city: '[there have been] some positive results in the development of new city districts... but it was a big fight and could not be pushed through in other areas... The main problem is the expensive land prices' (civil society respondent). LA21 is noted in the interviews (by both civil society and local government respondents) as being active and appreciated by participating interest organizations. However, it is also suggested that LA21 is not powerful within the local authority.

The relevant questionnaire responses are on public transport, climate protection and working with business. For public transport, 81 per cent said that the local authority is improving public transport to a high or very high extent; 55 per cent said that the local authority is improving on the adoption of climate change policies and strategies to a high or very high extent; and on the issue of working in partnership with business for sustainable development, the response rate was 60 per cent.

For the sum index of all environmental responses, the average, like Hanover, is fairly high at 2.8. For the economic and social indexes, the averages are slightly lower, but still high (2.5 for both indexes).

Dunkerque Urban Community, France (European Sustainable Cities and Towns Award Winner 1997)

The Dunkerque Urban Community (DUC) has a population of 215,000. The DUC is situated by the North Sea (close to the Belgian border). It is the third biggest commercial harbour in France. Since the end of World War II, the Dunkerque area has experienced heavy industrial development. Fifty-four per cent of the active population is employed in one of the 900 industries existing on the DUC territory. Twenty-six per cent of the industries are related to steel industry/metallurgy, 10 per cent to construction, 5 per cent to energy, and 4 per cent to chemistry. Although there are recognized health and environmental concerns linked to the predominance of the industrial sector in Dunkerque, employment opportunities also depend to a high degree upon industrial development.

The DUC is a municipal organization representing 18 individual local authorities surrounding the city of Dunkerque. This type of structure is privileged by national law. Urban communities have the role of defining the main political orientations and strategies for the territory that they represent. A key focus of the local authority is on managing risk and linking this to sustainable development. The DUC won the Sustainable Cities and Towns Award in 1997 and has sustainable development as a principal objective. The relevant documents are the *Agglomeration Contract*, which integrates sustainability issues, and *Sustainable Development Actors' Guide* (Dunkerque Urban Community Local Authority, 2002a, b). This latter seems particularly innovative as it sets out a methodology for sustainability to be implemented by those in local government and by civil society organizations.

The interviews cite a number of environmental actions, as well as social and economic actions related to the environment. In 1993 the DUC set up the Industrial Environment Scheme, linked to an environmental industrial plan. The local authority has developed initiatives around renewable energy and has a number of transport initiatives, such as buses running on gas, DUC employees using electric cars and the *Mobility Plan*, which aims to improve public transport and cycle facilities. The local authority promotes fair trade issues and has an urban renewal initiative (Project Neptune) that focuses on social and economic policies for deprived areas. One particular area of progress cited is the local authority employing local people in 'Green' areas – for example, in waste management. Responses from both local government and civil society particularly refer to the examples of energy-efficient transport, although there is still general concern about the issues of industrial pollution and risk.

The questionnaire responses on transport reflect the positive perceptions in the interviews: 73 per cent responded that the local authority is reducing the need to travel to a high/very high extent, and the figure is 54 per cent for the provision of pedestrian and cycling facilities. Seventy-two per cent perceived the local authority as addressing social equity issues in policy implementation to a high or very high extent. The 'average' for the environmental outcomes index is 2.4 and for economic outcomes it is 2.5; but it is highest for social issues (2.8), and this reflects the opinions of interviewees on progress in the social area.

Ottignies-Louvain La Neuve, Belgium (reference case study)

Ottignies-Louvain La Neuve was originally two towns, with Louvain La Neuve a university town that featured a high tradition of participation. The current population of the combined towns is 40,000. The university owns most of the land in the municipality, and this has implications for the areas in which (and the extent to which) the local government can act. The town has a *Charter for a Sustainable Development*. Other relevant documents are the *Political Declaration*, with sustainability as the basis for action, and the *Mobility Plan*, which states a number of specific actions (Ottignies-Louvain la Neuve Local Authority, 2001, 2002).

The interview respondents cite several areas of progress in the social and environment arenas – in particular, the *Mobility Plan* and projects emanating from this, such as cycle paths and assisting with mobility for excluded groups. Other areas of action are the provision of social housing, waste management and eco-procurement. There is some agreement between local government and civil society respondents on the level of progress, although the latter are less positive about what is perceived as the small scale of these actions.

The questionnaires show both local government and civil society perceiving transport as an area where the city is acting. Fifty per cent responded that the local authority provides facilities for pedestrians and cyclists to a high/very high extent. The figure is 68 per cent for the local authority reducing the need to travel, and 84 per cent for public transport provision. Fifty-seven per cent cited the local authority as being committed to eco-procurement to a high or very high extent. The sum index for the environment questions shows an 'average' of 2.7, while the figures are slightly lower for social aspects (2.3) and economic aspects (2.4)

Haarlem, The Netherlands (reference case study)

Haarlem faces particular environmental pressures due to heavy urbanization, a high density of population (150,000 people) and flood risks related to climate change. The local authority's focus is on environmental management, and, according to the fieldwork findings, urban planning is integrating sustainable development aspects, although it is not explicitly called sustainable development. The key documents are the *Strategic Plan*, which focuses on socio-economic issues but also takes account of environmental issues – for example, improving green spaces – and housing construction. The *Environmental Policy Plan 2003–2006* has a 'sustainability vision' and environmental goals, and the *Development Programme* is related to the *Strategic Plan*, but sets out a range of actions from this (Municipality of Haarlem, 1999a, b, 2003).

The main actions cited in the interviews are the separation of industrial from housing activities; recycling; cycling routes; improving soil quality; creation of green spaces; energy efficiency awareness-raising; noise pollution; and eco-procurement. One example of the local authority dealing with economic issues in relation to the environment is that of working with business on green spaces for industrial parks. A general concern from both local government and civil society sectors is the increase in car usage and the impact on emissions, although both agree that some progress in environmental aspects is occurring.

In the relevant questionnaire responses, 38 per cent thought that the local authority is providing and protecting green spaces to a high extent. On transport issues, 17 per cent said that the local authority is reducing the need to travel to a high or very high extent, and 27 per cent answered that it is providing public transport to a high extent. The higher response on provision of cycling and pedestrian facilities (58 per cent) reflects the emphasis in some of the interviews on these topics. On the issue of the local authority working in partnership with business and industry, 42 per cent responded that this is happening to a high or very high extent. The average for the environmental outcomes index is 2.2, with similar averages for the economic index (2.4) and the social aspects (2.3).

TOP FIVE CASE STUDIES IN SOUTHERN EUROPE

Calvià, Spain (LASALA Good Practice)

Calvià is a municipality of 50,000 inhabitants on the island of Majorca, but the population increases to 200,000 during the summer months. Calvià's landscape is characterized by a heavily urbanized coastline, but also a rural/mountainous protected zone which takes up 85 per cent of the territory. Calvià faces the issues characteristic of a heavily developed tourist zone: water consumption; waste discharge from boats; energy consumption; soil; and land-use pressures. Public transport is well developed (at least in the town of Palma); but the existence of an extensive network of large roads around Calvià promotes the use of private cars.

The LA21 of Calvià, led by the previous mayor (before the local elections in spring 2003 and also prior to the fieldwork taking place), was the driving force for any action led by the local authority. The Calvià *LA21 Action Plan* is the strategic plan for the municipality (Municipality of Calvià, 1994). Every single action taken by the municipality up until the local elections in 2003 was in the framework of LA21. The mayor was the direct political figure responsible for the project. The aim was to lead actions on environmental issues first, then on social issues, then, finally, to work on economic issues. Only actions related to the two first phases were achieved (environment and social) by the time of the elections.

For Calvià, the interviews were seen by the fieldworker as providing the most reliable source data for the project, as the leading political party in Calvià had just changed before the fieldwork was conducted, and it was therefore difficult to find the relevant people to complete the questionnaires. It was also more complex to assess whether the responses in the questionnaires referred to the 'now' or to the policies before the change in political power. In the interviews, the main areas of environmental progress cited are the creation of new green areas where hotels had been demolished; decreasing water usage and waste; cleaning up beaches; improving recycling; the building of the 'Calvià way', involving the creation of cycle and pedestrian paths and linking neighbourhoods (and also incorporating 'green' ideas in terms of the use of rainwater); and working with hotels on environmental improvements.

Social areas are also cited in terms of the creation of IFOC – a local employment agency for sustainable development jobs – and a 'social cooperation' initiative with elderly and disabled people. Although the focus has been on the environmental and social dimensions, interviewees also noted important progress being made in terms of economic aspects, such as working in partnership with hotels to develop sustainable tourism, and the promotion of the eco-tax for both residents and tourists. Both local government and civil society sectors comment that LA21 has been central to the work of Calvià, as the LA21 strategy and principles derived from this form the basis for policy-making in all areas. The sum indexes for environmental, economic and social outcomes (although less reliable in this instance) show an average of 2.3, 2.8 and 2.3, respectively; but these do not accurately reflect the situation in Calvià, where the environmental and social aspects were areas in which most progress has been made.

Ferrara, Italy (LASALA Good Practice)

Ferrara is a city in the northern part of Italy with a population of 133,000 inhabitants. The city has a rich cultural and historical heritage and the city centre is a protected United Nations Educational, Scientific and Cultural Organization (UNESCO) site, with a large pedestrian area. Ferrara was not part of the industrial 'boom' of the 1950s and 1960s (unlike other cities in the region), and there has been a focus on 'quality tourism' and, more recently, 'sustainable tourism'. There are close links between the province and city of Ferrara in relation to sustainable development implementation.

In the interviews, the main areas of progress in the environmental arena that are cited are eco-vehicles, cycle routes, the building of a methane plant to increase the level of renewable energy for the city, monitoring of air pollution, and protection of green spaces. In terms of policy tools, the province is a project partner in the Eco-budget Initiative (funded through the EU). It aims to take this initiative further by making eco-budgeting a legal requirement so that the administration has to adopt policies to accord with this. The civil society responses are generally supportive of the province approach to sustainable development, and they also mention the importance of the LA21 forum, with the initiatives that 'spin off' from the process.

From the questionnaire data on transport, 70 per cent of all respondents said that the local authority is taking action to reduce the need to travel to a high or very high extent. Seventy-one per cent said that the local authority is improving public transport, and 77 per cent that it is improving cyclist and pedestrian facilities. On climate protection issues, 47 per cent said that the local authority is addressing climate change concerns in its strategies and policies. These responses seem to reflect the interviewees' perceptions of where progress is being made. The questionnaire responses also show a very high proportion: 90 per cent believed that the local authority is using new policy delivery tools to achieve sustainable development to a high/very high extent, with a high proportion (64 per cent) perceiving these tools as effective. Sixty-four per cent thought that the local authority is committed to using environmental criteria in its procurement policies. For the environmental sum indexes, the 'average' is again fairly high, at 2.6, and is also high for social and economic questions (2.5 and 2.6, respectively), reflecting the perception in the interviews that action is taking place across all three dimensions of sustainability.

Barcelona Province, Spain (European Sustainable Cities and Towns Award Winner 1999)

The province of Barcelona is, effectively, a regional level of government. It covers 310 diverse local authorities, and takes measures to compensate for local deficiencies in some of these. The province acts as a network for municipalities but does not have direct implementation policies with regard to the local authorities within its jurisdiction. It is responsible for supporting and funding the LA21 programme for the province and has developed an LA21 model for all local authorities to use in developing their own sustainable development strategies and policies.

The main areas of progress in developing and applying the LA21 model are in terms of environmental management – specifically, waste collection and waste management, and water management. The province has also developed an environmental audits programme for local authorities to use, and a model LA21 for schools has been developed. The other main area of progress through the LA21 model is in terms of environmental purchasing. The interview responses indicate a high level of agreement between local government and civil society on the 'richness of the network association'; however, there is a general concern that more action is needed through LA21, particularly in the areas of integrating planning and land use. A representative from the business sector commented specifically on the need for joint agreements between business, other civil society sectors and local authorities (linking to the Johannesburg Type 2 agreements).

The relevant questionnaire responses on tools for policy delivery reflect the emphasis in the interviews on the LA21 model and on environmental purchasing. seventy per cent thought that the local authority is using policy tools to a high or very high extent; 59 per cent thought that these are very effective; and 57 per cent cited the use of environmental criteria in procurement policies to a high or very high extent. In terms of the sum index for all environmental questions, the average is 2.3, with slightly lower figures for economic and social aspects (1.9 and 2.1, respectively). This seems to reflect the environmental emphasis in the LA21 model.

Modena Province, Italy (LASALA Good Practice)

The city of Modena and its province has a population of 640,000 and is one of the most affluent areas in Italy, with a strong economic sector that is based predominantly on small local businesses. The province of Modena is characterized by its innovative and proactive approach to management and planning, and it has been a forerunner of LA21 in Italy. The relationship between the province and the local authorities within it (the city of Modena being one of these) appears to be less developed than in the Ferrara case in terms of sustainable development implementation.

The main areas of progress, according to the interviews, are the provision of heating systems to improve energy efficiency; energy saving; waste reduction; and environmental education. The province is aiming for an environmental budget within two years, based on a European model. In the arena of economic sustainability, the interviews cited the encouragement of SMEs to adopt EMAS. There are 60,000 small businesses in the province, so potentially this could have a substantial impact. The key policy tools are EMAS and LA21. The latter is seen as assisting with progress in the areas of energy saving and environmental education (particularly in terms of raising awareness in civil society). Both civil society and local government respondents comment on the importance of LA21 in pushing the process forward, and LA21 continues to have an important input into the province urban planning policy. However, local government respondents note the need for the local authority to set a good example on environmental protection, such as energy saving in public buildings.

In terms of climate change aspects in the questionnaire responses, 68 per cent believed that the local authority is addressing climate change concerns in its strategies and policies. The responses to the three policy tool questions in the questionnaire show that 86 per cent perceived the local authority as using new policy tools to a high or very high extent; however, only 38 per cent saw these as improving policy delivery to the same degree. 35 per cent thought that the local authority is using environmental criteria in procurement policies effectively. For the environmental and economic sum indexes, the averages are 2.5 and 2.8, and for social outcomes it is 2.2, suggesting that the economic and environmental aspects predominate.

Santa Perpetua de Mogoda, Spain (LASALA Good Practice)

Santa Perpetua is one of the local authorities within Barcelona Province. With a population of 20,000, it has traditionally been a wealthy industrial town. As it lies within Barcelona Province, the main document for sustainable development is the LA21 plan, which is linked to the environment plan, with a number of associated actions.

The key areas of progress as cited in the interviews are 'good housekeeping' for waste within the local authority – specifically, improving recycling – and developing a composting network in the municipality: 'In the last six years the whole technical department has been impregnated with the sustainability message from the little actions (for example, reusing paper in everyday activities) to the big projects.' Other areas cited are the improvement of public pathways and cycle facilities, and the use of sustainability criteria in public buildings. The local authority has also created a Regional Association for Ecology. In terms of policy tools, Santa Perpetua de Mogoda uses the LA21 model from Barcelona, and the local authority is working to make LA21 the structural framework for all departmental policies. The responses indicate a broad agreement in both local government and civil society that the LA21 model provides a 'meaningful' process for sustainable development policy implementation.

The most relevant issue in the questionnaire responses is transport – with 35 per cent saying that the local authority is improving facilities for cyclists/pedestrians to a high or very high extent. Sixty-three per cent perceived that the local authority is using new tools for sustainable development to a high or very high extent; 44 per cent responded that these tools are influencing the delivery of policies. Meanwhile, 66 per cent said that the local authority is committed to a high or very high extent to using environmental criteria in its procurement policies. For the sum index of environmental questions, the average is 2.6. It is slightly higher for the economic questions (2.8), but lower for social issues (2.4).

TOP FIVE CASE STUDIES IN NORTHERN EUROPE

Gotland, Sweden (LASALA Good Practice)

The island of Gotland, including the capital Visby, was the location for the fieldwork. The island has a population of 57,000, but this rises to 700,000 during the summer months. The island markets itself as an 'eco-municipality' – in Sweden this means a focus on developing a community characterized by the aim of achieving sustainability and economical use of resources. The fieldworker noted a sense of island 'togetherness', and a focus on self-sufficiency, nature and culture. Environmental policy outcomes are high on the agenda of the local authority. One area for which Gotland is particularly noted is the use of wind power. The key documents are Agenda 21 – an eco-programme – as well as sustainable development. Within this the stated aim is to become a zero-emission zone through the efficient use of water, energy, land and materials, with the overarching objective to achieve sustainable development in one generation.

The interview responses highlight many areas of progress in terms of environmental protection. The city is a member of KLIMP (the Nordic equivalent of the Climate Alliance). It is active in the area of waste management, renewable energy and, specifically, in implementing the Green Flag project (using renewable energy solutions in schools/day-care centres, with the aim of all these institutions becoming environmentally certified). The local authority has introduced land-use policies aimed at protecting green areas, and it promotes the use of environmentally friendly buses. The local government and civil society responses indicate a high level of consensus between these sectors on the nature and level of progress in Gotland, and the civil society sectors are supportive of the local authority in their responses. In particular, the importance of being an 'eco-municipality' is noted by both sets of respondents.

The questionnaire responses on limiting the use of green-field land in development also show a high proportion perceiving progress in this area – with 88 per cent responding that this is occurring to a high or very extent. On climate protection, 69 per cent responded that the local authority is addressing climate change concerns in strategies and policies to a high or very high extent, and 53 per cent said that it is reducing greenhouse gases to a high or very high extent. In terms of policy tools, the key examples cited in the interviews are the environmental purchasing policy and the integration of LA21 within policy processes. The questionnaire responses show 33 per cent as saying that the local authority is using new tools for policy delivery for sustainable development to a high or very high extent, and the same percentage on the success of these policies. On eco-procurement, the figure is higher at 57 per cent. For the sum index of all environmental responses, the average is fairly high – 2.6 – and 2.5 and 2.4, respectively, for the economic and social aspects.

Albertslund, Denmark (European Sustainable Cities and Towns Award Winner 1996)

Albertslund is a suburb municipality of Copenhagen, with 30,000 residents. Many university students live here and commute to the capital city for college. The town is fairly new, and those who moved there originally built it up themselves and are highly educated. There appears to be political consensus behind the implementation of sustainable development. The interviews cite a number of actions in the environmental arena: green accounts for residential areas; the local authority ceasing the use of pesticides throughout the municipality; and 'eco-food' in 95 per cent of local authority institutions (schools and day-care centres), linked into the Green Flag initiative for ecological day-care centres and schools. Other aspects include improving energy efficiency through more environmentally friendly heating systems. The local government and civil society respondents all noted progress in these areas; in particular, civil society respondents emphasized the clear interest of the local authority in becoming more sustainable.

One local government respondent noted that the beginning of a process is easier: 'We pick the fruits from the bottom first', and as the process proceeds, stronger efforts are needed to progress further. This is evident in the example of carbon dioxide reduction being achieved, but with more energy being consumed, particularly through the increased use of cars. One respondent noted: 'In the end, it calls for a change in living habits... therefore, the dialogue with the inhabitants will become more and more important in the future'.

The questionnaire responses also reflect the perception that Albertslund is making progress in a number of topic areas. Eighty-seven per cent responded that the local authority is improving or developing pedestrian and cyclist facilities to a high or very high extent; 67 per cent that the local authority is addressing climate protection issues in its strategies and policies; and 56 per cent said that the local authority is addressing social equity issues in its policy agenda and implementation. On the issue of working with business, 82 per cent responded that the local authority is promoting environmentally friendly working practices in business to a high or very high extent.

In terms of policy tools, Albertslund (according to the interviews and from the fieldworker perspective) has an active LA21 process and LA21 centre. Sustainability achievements are seen to be enhanced by the process, due partly to the active Agenda 21 centre, which was originally started by the inhabitants. The local authority has EMAS in several departments and is aiming for all departments to be certified by the year 2008. In the questionnaire responses, the perceptions reflect those in the interviews: 92 per cent said that the local authority is using new policy tools to a high or very high extent and 86 per cent thought that the impact of these is high or very high. The sum indexes for environment, economic and social questions show averages of 2.5, 2.8 and 2.3, respectively.

Stavanger, Norway (LASALA Good Practice)

Stavanger has a population of 110,000. During the past ten years it has become a forerunner city in energy issues, and was the first Norwegian city to have a climate and energy plan. The city has a long tradition of working with sustainability ideas (through a focus on environmental sustainability). The environmental plan for the city dates to 1991, so it was a 'forerunner' for sustainability in Norway. Stavanger is the 'oil city' of Norway and is a wealthy city, featuring large companies. The local authority is currently re-planning the city, and linked to this, it is focusing on the development and improvement of green areas and on measures to reduce traffic.

The key documents are the *Climate and Energy Plan* and the *Environmental Plan*, which are being implemented through strategic planning for the city (Municipality of Stavanger, 1996, 2001). The interviews have cited a number of areas of progress – mainly in the environmental arena. Stavanger, like Gotland, is a member of KLIMP and mobility issues are addressed through planning policy and, specifically, transport planning. The respondents suggest that there is a focus on re-planning the city, including the creation of green areas, and on traffic reduction. Energy efficiency (for example, heating systems) and waste management are also cited as key areas of progress. The local authority has a purchasing policy, whereby 10 per cent more is paid by the local authority for work or goods produced within the municipality if it meets certain environmental requirements. Both local government and civil society respondents suggest that LA21 in the city is important to progress, as it is linking the two major environmental NGOs, the local authority and business in policy implementation.

From the questionnaire responses, 61 per cent said that the local authority is limiting the use of green-field land to a high or very high extent, and 72 per cent that it is safeguarding or creating open spaces. On transport issues, the figures are 83 per cent that there are substantial improvements with regards to pedestrian and cyclist facilities and 47 per cent that progress has been made with improving public transport. On climate protection issues, 50 per cent responded that the local authority is addressing climate protection in its policies and strategies to a high or very high extent.

In terms of economic issues, interviewees cited cooperation between local authority and business through a number of formal mechanisms. In the questionnaires, 44 per cent perceived the local authority as promoting environmental issues in business to a high or very high extent, and 50 per cent perceived the local authority as working in partnership with business. As noted above, in the area of policy tools, Stavanger has an environmental purchasing policy, and it is also observed to have a very active LA21 process. However, the questionnaire responses show fairly low percentages – 39 per cent said that the local authority is using new policy tools to a high or very high extent, while 17 per cent saw these as having a high impact. A higher figure – 50 per cent – cited the use of environmental criteria in procurement policies to a high or very high extent.

The sum indexes for environmental, economic and social outcomes show similar averages – 2.5 for the former two aspects, and 2.4 on social aspects.

Växjö, Sweden (LASALA Good Practice)

Växjö is a university town with a population of 76,000. The fieldworker described it as an 'idyllic' place, with a high proportion of open space. The key relevant documents are LA21 and the *Environment Policy* (Municipality of Växjö, 1996). One of the main areas of progress, as highlighted in the interviews, is energy efficiency. Växjö is a 'fossil fuel-free' city – linked to an initiative promoted by national government. This involves adopting the aim of reducing fossil fuel emissions by 50 per cent by 2010, and is based on cooperation between the local authority, university and private sector. Växjö is also a pilot city for the National Nature Protection Association, and another notable action has been the cleaning of a major lake in the municipality. The local authority, like Ferrara in Italy, is a project partner in the Eco-budget Initiative, funded through the EU. The local government and civil society respondents concur on the importance of being a 'fossil fuel-free' city and on being chosen as a pilot for the nature protection initiative.

The questionnaire responses on the areas of safeguarding or enlarging public open spaces show that 83 per cent feel the local authority is making progress to a high or very high extent. On the issue of addressing climate change concerns in policies and strategies, the figure is 100 per cent. For the sum indexes of environmental questions the average is 2.9, reflecting, perhaps, progress on environmental aspects, although it is also fairly high for economic factors and for social aspects (both at 2.6).

Tampere, Finland (European Sustainable Cities and Towns Award Winner 1999)

Tampere has a population of 200,000, making it the third largest city in Finland. It was traditionally an industrial city; but now research, culture and education are important, most probably linked to it being a university city. The city is developing rapidly and has an increasing population; however it also has the lowest crime rates in the country.

Tampere is a member of Eurocities. Sustainable development is explicitly stated in the core strategies for the city: *The Sustainable Development Report* (revised every two years), which evaluates how sustainability targets in the environmental management system are achieved (this aspect is a national government requirement). The most recent *Environmental Strategy* has all aspects of sustainability highly integrated (City of Tampere, 2003a, b). This strategy is one of six strategies that form part of the environmental management system. Actions in the *Environmental Strategy* include an internet guide on the environment for citizens, a recycling programme and a campaign on energy saving.

The interviews reveal perceptions of progress primarily regarding environmental aspects. The local authority has achieved progress on waste management (recycling), renewable energy and energy efficiency. With regard to the latter, the local authority set up an energy centre; it has changed to heating from natural gas, and has policies to reduce carbon dioxide emissions. Both local government and civil society respondents have similar views on where actions have occurred – particularly in terms of the environmental management system, although a general concern is that the economy is driving policies and that car use is increasing.

The questionnaire responses on climate protection show that 60 per cent thought that the local authority is addressing climate change to a high or very high extent in its strategies and policies. However, only 20 per cent believed that the local authority is highly successful in reducing greenhouse gas emissions. Sixty-seven per cent said that the local authority is using new policy tools to a high or very high extent, although only 22 per cent responded that this has had an impact. For the sum index of environmental questions, the average is 2.4; for the economic index the figure is 2.2; and for the social index the average is 2.2.

CONCLUSIONS

The main emphasis in the material relating to policy outcomes has inevitably been on environmental sustainability, as the majority of achievements in policy and practice are taking place in the environmental field. In terms of the Aalborg Principles (and the subsequent Aalborg Commitments produced in June 2004), the policy achievements identified in this research show that local authorities are seriously addressing a number of key sustainability issues: the establishment of urban management schemes for improving sustainability; the preservation of natural common goods (through the use of renewable energy sources, energy efficiency measures and protection of green areas); sustainable transport; a vibrant (and sustainable) local economy; and the consideration of local to global links. The environmental emphasis is to be expected as it relates to local authorities having the most freedom and opportunity to act on environmental s. In some instances, the environmental arena may be seen as the most urgent – for example, in terms of managing risk or mitigating the effects of industrial pollution; in other cases, environmental sustainability is seen as the route through which to tackle social equity and economic development issues. However, there clearly are towns and cities that are moving towards an integrative approach to sustainable development, incorporating social and economic dimensions in a range of innovative policies and projects.

The case studies represent a range of local government types, but also of population sizes, from 3000 in Dunajska Luzna to 1.3 million in cities such as Munich. Population, however, was not a primary criterion for selection, although we were aware that this could be a factor in achieving sustainable development. In fact, the findings do not indicate a clear correlation between the size of population and extent of progress, and we are therefore not able to state that a certain size of town or city is more likely to lead to sustainable development policy outcomes. Bigger cities undoubtedly have access to more resources, and may be able to attract higher calibre officers and politicians. Conversely, smaller municipalities may be closer to their citizens and have more opportunities to develop an effective working relationship between the local authority and civil society organizations. This leads us into a discussion of the factors and conditions for sustainable development progress, considered in Chapter 4.

Chapter 4

Institutional Capacity and Social Capacity

INTRODUCTION

This chapter continues the analysis of the empirical material and focuses on the independent variables or 'process' aspects in the research. Here, the findings from the interview material on institutional capacity, social capacity and capacity-building for sustainable development in the 40 case studies are presented. These findings relate to the 'process' aspects in the Aalborg Charter – the relevant Principles being the incorporation of sustainability principles within all local authority policies and practices; resolving problems by working with other municipalities, sub-national and national government; and involving citizens and stakeholder organizations in delivering sustainability policies.

The analysis concentrates initially on institutional capacity in the local authority case studies in terms of the factors and conditions for sustainable development policy achievement. Consideration is then given to social capacity in relation to sustainable development, and particularly the influence and role of those organizations/interest groups which seem to be most engaged in the sustainability processes of the 40 case studies. The third aspect considered in this chapter, and of central importance to the research, is capacity-building for sustainable development. As explained in earlier chapters, we are interested in the nature and extent of capacity-building for sustainable development in terms of approaches and tools used by local authorities to engage civil society in activities and policy processes for sustainable development.

The interview material provides evidence on the following aspects:

- the different ways in which institutional capacity within local government is developed and maintained;
- the nature of social capacity in civil society (and specifically in the organizations and groups involved in sustainable development policy processes);
- the devices and tools employed by local government to build capacity within civil society and local authorities.

The presentation of the material differs slightly from Chapter 3. Examples of institutional capacity and capacity-building are in tabular form (showing the names of the case studies against each example); but the social capacity section is explained only through text, due to the smaller amount of material collected. Any innovative examples are noted in the discussion of the material. The same ranking mechanism employed in Chapter 3 is then used to identify the top case studies in the four regions and to present the key capacity factors in each of these.

INSTITUTIONAL CAPACITY

Table 4.1 presents examples of institutional capacity that emerged in the interviews and indicates the case studies where these were explicitly noted.

Table 4.1 *Institutional capacity*

Committed officers	• Officers across departments highly educated and motivated, linking to innovation (*Dunkerque Urban Community; Tampere*) • Professional and technical expertise (*Barcelona Province*) • Specific individuals as key to sustainability process (*Dunkerque Urban Community; Gdansk; Falkenberg; Granollers*) • Strong team of officers (*Durham County Council; Beja*) • Diversity of ages and younger officers (*Munich; Anyksciai; Växjö*)
Political will	• Political continuity and stability within a 'Red–Green' coalition (*Hanover; Munich; Dunkerque; Calvià; Santa Perpetua de Mogoda; Ferrara*) • Central role of mayor (*Ottignies-Louvain la Neuve; Barcelona Province; Haarlem; Celle Ligure; Valenciennes; Dunajska Luzna*) • Role of senior politicians (vice-mayors) (*Beja; Celle Ligure; Anyksciai; Haarlem*) • Political consensus for sustainability agenda (*Stavanger; Gotland*)
Training for sustainable development	• Environmental action programme, including training courses (*Dunajska Luzna*) • Senior officer training (*Dunkerque Urban Community*) • Officer training (*Kuressaare; Orastie*) • Sustainable development methodology (*Dunkerque Urban Community*) • Training for politicians (*London Borough of Redbridge*) • Inter-departmental training (*Dungannon and South Tyrone; Dunkerque Urban Community*) • Specific and substantial budget allocated for training (*Haarlem*)

Table 4.1 *(continued)*

Mainstreaming into working practices	• Environment budget details sustainability issues (*Vantaa*) • Green purchasing integrated across departments (*Ferrara; Stavanger*) • Networked services between directorates (*Hanover*) • Sustainability principles integrated within departments operations (*Stirling*) • Integration of LA21 at all levels (*Gotland; Calvià*) • LA21 process assisting in developing cross-departmental links (*Dungannon and South Tyrone; Fano*)
National and international networks/activities	• Eco-municipality (*Växjö; Gotland; Falkenberg*) • Eurocities member (*Tampere; Thessaloniki*) • Member of Balkan Cities and Med-Cities (*Thessaloniki*) • Participation in conferences (*Gdansk; Lahti*)
'Province'-level support and networks	• 'Province'-level support for LA21 (*Ferrara; Modena Province; Barcelona Province*) • Network of municipalities for LA21 (*South-west Finland Agenda*) • Conglomeration of local authorities under statutory legislation (*Dunkerque Urban Community*)

In a number of the case studies, both representatives of civil society organizations, and local authority officers and politicians cite the importance of having officers who committed to the principles of sustainability and to what could be termed a 'public service ethos' – that is, working for a local authority. Of particular interest are the comments on the willingness of decision-makers to be innovative, implementing sustainable development policies, linked to a high level of knowledge and expertise on the relevant issues. The existence of highly educated staff is also connected to higher motivation levels. Moreover, interviews cite the importance of having strong teams of multi-skilled officers working in this area. This is seen as beneficial, particularly in implementing the more 'pioneering' ideas on aspects, such as Green purchasing.

A number of case studies highlight the role of individual officers in progressing with sustainable development. In Dunkerque Urban Community (France) it is noted that the president is active on sustainable development; in Gdansk (Poland), the head of environmental protection is perceived as a key individual in promoting sustainability, particularly in relation to tourism; and Falkenberg (Sweden) has a well-known and well-regarded Local Agenda 21 (LA21) officer, who is perceived to be the strongest link between civil society and local government.

In several case studies – Munich (Germany), Växjö (Sweden) and Anyksciai (Lithuania) – it has been suggested that a diversity of ages of officers and the employment of younger officers benefit the sustainable development process and help to develop capacity in this area. A notable comment in Växjö is that there is a 'learning' culture within the local authority: 'People within the authorities are ambitious and curious and, with that, are open to ideas.'

In terms of political commitment, the interview responses reveal two related aspects: the commitment of a political party to sustainability principles and action; and political will in the form of individual politicians – in particular, an 'entrepreneurial' mayor. There are a number of case studies where political stability and continuity is cited as being crucial to sustainable development policy achievement (and this is often linked to a 'Red–Green' political coalition). Interviewees also emphasize the role of senior politicians, in addition to the mayor.

Many of the case studies have training programmes or courses specifically related to environmental sustainability or, more broadly, to sustainable development, both for officers and politicians. One notable example is that of Dunkerque Urban Community, which has a Sustainable Development Methodology developed by the local authority. This links into training on sustainability and is perceived as leading to improved institutional capacity for sustainability. Haarlem (The Netherlands) is the only case study where there is an explicit and substantial budget allocated specifically for training on sustainability issues, and it is interesting to note that interviewees in Haarlem link this high level of training to higher motivation levels.

'Mainstreaming' sustainability is understood in this research as integrating principles of sustainable development within the institutional culture and working practices of a local authority, and transferring this into actions. The interviews reveal a number of examples of mainstreaming sustainable development – for instance, in Vantaa (Finland) the perception is that the environmental profile has improved through the work of the environment department, and through the local authority budget explicitly detailing sustainable development issues. Several case studies have inter-departmental collaboration on sustainability issues, and there are also examples of sustainability principles being integrated within a number of departments.

Several of the cases mention the role of LA21 in the mainstreaming of sustainability. In Gotland (Sweden) LA21 is integrated within the working of all levels of the municipality, and in Dungannon and South Tyrone (UK) LA21 is seen as assisting with developing cross-departmental links. Finally, in Fano (Italy), although there is no LA21 action plan at this stage, many people see the LA21 process, currently underway, as being an important tool in promoting greater collaboration between the different departments of the local authority. It is envisaged that the management of the LA21 process by the cultural department should help to promote a solution involving greater cross-sectoral integration, as it will not be identified as 'belonging to the environment department'.

The role of national and international networks for sustainable development is perceived as important in a number of the case studies. Falkenberg engages in many 'networking' activities at national and international level and, like Växjö and Gotland, it has taken the initiative to become an 'eco-municipality' and is a member of SEKO – the Swedish eco-municipality network. Thessaloniki (Greece) participates in many European networks – for example, Eurocities, Med-Cities and Balkan Cities; however, this is perceived as being due to politicians having little power to effect change within the city itself and needing to seek ideas on good practice from other cities.

Two of the case studies (Barcelona Province and South-west Finland Agenda) could be described as 'networks' set up principally to support local authorities in developing their LA21 processes and programmes for action. The Barcelona model of LA21 provides technical, political and financial support for local authorities. This approach of developing and disseminating the LA21 model to local authorities is perceived by respondents as beneficial due to the technical support and financial assistance provided. At the provincial level, each person within the environmental service is responsible for directing an LA21 process in at least one of the municipalities in the province. The province is active in promoting sustainability, through working groups, publications, conferences, exchange of good practice, and disseminating the LA21 model. It also has links with two European networks in the environmental arena. The second, South-west Finland Agenda, is a voluntary network of small neighbouring municipalities, formed around the city of Turku/Åbo, in Finland, and coordinated by an officer in the environment department of Turku/Åbo. This network is intended to support the smaller municipalities in terms of resources for sustainable development policy development and implementation.

SOCIAL CAPACITY

The existence, nature and impact of social capital or capacity on sustainable development mainstreaming and progress is clearly a complex area, as discussed at length in Chapter 2. The focus in the research has been on tangible evidence of social capacity through examining the role and influence of civil society organizations and interest groups within a municipality, rather than individual citizens per se. The main sectors that appear to have most involvement in, and links to, the local authorities in the 40 cases are the local media (primarily newspapers, and mainly in the Northern European case studies), business, industry, universities and (largely environmental) non-governmental organizations (NGOs). Several examples are given below.

In Munich it is noted by a civil society organization that the influence of the local media is very high, with five daily newspapers reporting on civic engagement and publicizing local activities, and the perception in Stavanger (Norway) is that 'the influence of the media on local politics is very high and the media shape public opinion'. More specifically, in Calvià (Spain), Stavanger, Veliko Turnovo (Bulgaria), Hanover (Germany) and Tampere (Finland) interviewees cite the positive role of local newspapers and the local radio in spreading awareness about sustainable development.

Several quotes from different case studies highlight the perceived importance of the local media:

> Sustainable development on Gotland has a very high news value
> (local journalist).

> I myself learn about sustainable development from the news-
> papers, while communicating with the representatives of the
> administration of the city, within the process of solving practical
> issues (civil society organization in Korolev).

> [The media is a] local democracy tool… to get heard and try
> to influence the policy process (local authority respondent,
> Stavanger).

> The local newspaper in Albertslund is important as people read this
> regularly and it is published weekly. This provides an opportunity
> for an open debate and is very 'objective' and 'balanced' (local
> government respondent).

However, in other cases, such as Ferrara (Italy), and Thessaloniki, the concerns were that there was not enough involvement of the media or that it was controlled by central government or local government.

In many of the case studies the key sector is environmental NGOs. In Vantaa there is an umbrella organization for NGOs and all voluntary organizations, which is perceived by interviewees to reinforce the capacity of the individual organizations, and Falkenberg is perceived to have a high level of civic engagement in NGOs, including environmental organizations. In Calvià, the hotel industry is strongly involved in the implementation of environmental initiatives, while in Haarlem, Dubrovnik (Croatia), Munich and Lahti (Finland) specific businesses or business organizations have links with the local authority on sustainability projects, such as energy efficiency measures and green areas in business parks.

CAPACITY-BUILDING

Table 4.2 sets out examples of capacity-building cited in the interviews.

A high-profile approach to 'marketing' a municipality is mentioned in several cases, particularly in relation to cultural, educational and technological issues. Valenciennes (France) has a City Heart cultural project, while Frederikshavn (Denmark) has named itself City of Light (a way of trying to develop the cultural dimension and to encourage citizens to remain in the city rather than migrate). In Baia Mare (Romania) the local authority has labelled itself as a 'learning city' in relation to developing information technology and communications. Fano (Italy) has a less high-profile approach, in which two officers in the cultural department are promoting a vision of the city that puts children first. Following this vision of the *Città del Bambini*, they have promoted several sustainability initiatives, either as a direct or indirect consequence of these actions.

In terms of the establishment of centres and forums, there are two different issues here: first, the setting up of physical 'centres' for citizens and organizations to visit in order to find out about specific initiatives and projects about sustainability; and, second, the establishment of a variety of 'forums' for engaging with particular groups or citizens, in general.

Table 4.2 *Examples of capacity-building*

LA21 Capacity-building	• LA21 participation plan (*Santa Perpetua de Mogoda*) • LA21 methodology to involve civil society (*Barcelona Province*) • Strong partnership through LA21 (*Durham County Council*)
Marketing and promotion	• City Heart cultural project (*Valenciennes*) • City of Light promotion (*Frederikshavn*) • Città del Bambini (*Fano*)
Centre/forums	• Energy centre set up by local authority (*Tampere*) • Council of Sustainable Development for civil society organizations (*Dunkerque Urban Community*) • Munich Forum to encourage citizen engagement (*Munich*) • Citizens' commissions (*Granollers*) • Roundtable to discuss sustainable development issues (*Veliko Turnovo*) • Consumption Centre to inform civil society and provide Information – e.g. on recycling (*Lahti*) • Local authority funds environmental lab, supporting links between local authority and civil society groups on sustainability issues (*Fano*)
Information provision to civil society	• Training/seminars on sustainable development for civil society (*Barcelona Province*) • Information provided to civil society (e.g. website) (*Dubrovnik; Orastie*) • Website for citizens to measure ecological footprint (*Stavanger*) • Education of young people on sustainable development issues (*Albertslund*) • Green accounts for all residential areas to see what local authority has achieved each year (*Albertslund*)
Links with organized interests	• Local authority supporting development of civil society organizations – e.g. Green Day and Daily Life (*Stavanger*) • University cooperation (*Tampere; Växjö; Korolev; Santa Perpetua de Mogoda*) • Encouraging small and medium-sized enterprises (SMEs) to adopt Environmental Management Audit Schemes (EMAS) (*Modena Province*) • Working with business organizations on energy saving (*Frederikshavn*) • Expansive Växjö initiative, linking the local authority and businesses (*Växjö*)

In Fano, the local authority provides the office space and some limited funding for the eco-lab, which carries out environmental education and projects with schools. In Lahti and Tampere (Finland) the local authorities have established centres to inform people about environmental issues, such as energy efficiency and recycling, and on specific actions for individuals to make changes in support of environmental sustainability.

The forums take a number of guises – for instance, Dunkerque Urban Community has a Council of Sustainable Development that provides a platform of exchange and consultation on major plans for the main representatives of civil society organizations, while Gotland has an Environment Council, created as a discussion forum between local government and civil society. Granollers (Spain) has citizens' commissions where the city council exchanges ideas on sustainability and other issues with associations from different sectors.

In the area of education and information provision, the use of on-line technology is cited as important. In Dubrovnik the local authority website publishes information on its activities (including sustainable development) and encourages responses to this from citizens, while Stavanger has developed a website that allows people to measure their ecological footprint. In Orastie (Romania) the local authority has press conferences and 'Green pages' on its website to inform civil society about its progress with sustainability. A notable example is in Albertslund (Denmark), which has Green accounts for all residential areas (these are annual reports that residents can look at to see what the local authority is achieving in their area in relation to sustainability). In Falkenberg there is a high-profile and well-regarded LA21 unit that organizes courses on environmental sustainability. This unit also promotes the use of local products, delivers an environmental calendar to all households and provides all two-year olds with backpacks containing information on environment and health issues.

There is a number of examples of local authorities supporting and promoting the development of civil society organizations – for instance, through initiatives such as Green Daily Life and Greenday in Stavanger, as well as Stavanger's Green City initiative. In the majority of case studies where there is a university in the municipality – Korolev (Russia), Tampere (Finland), Santa Perpetua de Mogoda (Spain) and Växjö (Sweden) – there also seems to be a strong link between the local authority and individuals within the university. The university often supports the local authority in developing the sustainability agenda through providing expertise and advice on policy development and being involved in the relevant forums, as well as including sustainability aspects in the curriculum. In the South-west Finland Agenda there is cooperation between the local authorities and business organizations on energy-efficiency initiatives, and Durham County Council (UK) has a wide-ranging and active partnership, through LA21, which aims to involve business, community organizations and utilities (such as Northumberland Water).

The analysis now draws on the above findings in order to identify those case studies in which institutional capacity, social capacity and capacity-building are most evident and advanced.

TOP 18 CASE STUDIES FOR INSTITUTIONAL CAPACITY, SOCIAL CAPACITY AND CAPACITY-BUILDING

The intention was to have 20 'top' case studies in the same way as for the policy outcomes. However, having allocated scores for each of these aspects, four of those in Eastern Europe and two in Northern Europe at the lower end of the top 20 had identical scores. The decision, therefore, was made to just focus on the top *four* for these two regions, rather than to extend the analysis to a further four. These 18 cases are listed in Table 4.3 and are ordered according to their rank within each region (based on the *total* of the scores for institutional and social capacity, and capacity-building); they are then described in further detail below. The majority of these case studies are the same as those in the 'top 20' for policy outcomes.

Table 4.3 *Top 18 Case for institutional capacity, social capacity and capacity-building*

Case study	Institutional capacity	Social capacity	Capacity-building	Total
Eastern Europe				
Gdansk, Poland	7.5	10	10	**27.5**
Korolev, Russia	7.5	7.5	10	**25**
Dunajska Luzna, Slovakia	5	10	7.5	**22.5**
Kuressaare, Estonia	7.5	5	7.5	**20**
Western Europe				
Munich, Germany	15	15	15	**45**
Hanover, Germany	15	10	12.5	**37.5**
Dunkerque Urban Community, France	15	7.5	10	**32.5**
Haarlem, The Netherlands	15	7.5	10	**32.5**
Ottignies-Louvain la Neuve, Belgium	7.5	10	10	**27.5**
Southern Europe				
Calvià, Spain	15	10	10	**35**
Ferrara, Italy	15	10	15	**35**
Modena Province, Italy	10	12.5	12.5	**35**
Santa Perpetua de Mogoda, Spain	10	7.5	10	**27.5**
Barcelona Province, Spain	12.5	0	12.5	**25**
Northern Europe				
Gotland, Sweden	15	15	15	**45**
Albertslund, Denmark	15	12.5	15	**42.5**
Stavanger, Norway	15	7.5	15	**37.5**
Tampere, Finland	12.5	10	10	**32.5**

TOP FOUR CASE STUDIES IN EASTERN EUROPE

Gdansk, Poland

Respondents note good cross-departmental working and linking between officers and politicians, particularly the positive role of the environment department. The head of environmental protection is perceived as a key individual in promoting sustainability in terms of tourism. The fieldworker notes that this person is described as 'the engine behind the success... [she has] a good ability to convince others and show positive examples of sustainable development, helping her to gain the support from the city council'. There is recognition by civil society respondents of some environmental improvements; but these are perceived as small-scale projects – for example, the creation of cycle paths. In terms of capacity-building measures, the main tool is LA21, although currently the range of groups represented on the LA21 forum seems to be limited.

Korolev, Russia

Marketing itself as a 'science city', Korolev is cited as having a high proportion of educated people. In the local authority, there is no specific training for sustainable development; but respondents suggest the approach is 'learning by doing'. There is a perception that good cooperation exists between departments, with weekly meetings held to discuss policy development. The combination of a strategic plan and a mayor who is open to new ideas and methods is cited as positive for sustainable development. In terms of social capacity, the main interest organization influencing the development of sustainability policies seems to be scientists, and this group is perceived as having the respect of the local authority. Other activities are through schools organizing conferences on sustainability and environment issues, and the university is perceived to have a high involvement in the process. The level of capacity-building appears to be fairly high. Respondents note that the city administration is open to a dialogue with citizens, and that the distance between civil society and the local authority is narrowing. This is seen as a positive change. In particular, the positive links between the university and city government are noted and the local authority plays a proactive role in communicating with citizens (the mayor appearing at events, as one example) and in working with school children in developing the city.

Dunajska Luzna, Slovakia

In terms of institutional capacity, the Environmental Action Programme for the town includes a section on organizing courses on International Standards Organization (ISO) environmental standards and environmental impact assessments (EIAs) for both officers and politicians. In addition, the mayor is seen as an important driving force for sustainable development. The local authority has set up LA21 commissions to promote sustainability within civil society organizations, and the civil society responses suggest that the input of the university in terms of technical expertise is beneficial for the development of sustainable planning. According to a senior politician:

> Many civil society organizations are helping to direct Dunajska Luzna to be more sustainable; they are forming a mosaic of all relevant local issues... NGOs are our future and thanks to them

citizens in Dunajska Luzna are starting to change and are more open to new ideas.

Both civil society and local government respondents concur that there are still major problems to address, particularly improving infrastructure in the town; however, the Community Environmental Association, which includes the LA21 forum, is seen as an important link between local government and civil society.

Kuressaare, Estonia

Specialists in the local authority are seen as being well educated, innovative and ambitious. The city is keen to establish international contacts, and institutional culture is becoming more open to 'learning' about sustainability issues. The role of committed individuals – particularly officers – and a stable government are stated as important in this aspect. In terms of social capacity, there are noted to be many civil society organizations; but it is not clear whether there is active engagement by particular sectors of civil society or by specific organizations. One comment is that people are still learning to express their opinions and that, as part of a Soviet legacy, local government is not yet practised in how to communicate with its population. Due to this, there is currently a weak relationship between local government and civil society. However, there are some informal links developing between these that are cited as being important to developing the sustainability process.

TOP FIVE CASE STUDIES IN WESTERN EUROPE

Munich, Germany

One particular comment was the benefit of having young staff in mainstreaming sustainability. A further point made was that the political will, through the 'Red–Green' coalition, has led to department heads becoming more involved in sustainability issues, as each head is the Agenda 21 officer in their own department. In terms of social capital, responses from civil society refer to there being many intellectuals in the city who are open to the idea of sustainable development. Furthermore, the private sector cooperates on initiatives with the local authority. Civil society organizations are perceived to be well organized and articulate, and the interviews with these organizations revealed some criticism of the local authority approach; but there was support for the Agenda 21 office. A senior planning officer notes: 'The local politicians are very engaged in and care about the development of their city; this motivates high civic engagement.' One key example of capacity-building for citizens in the arena of sustainability is the Green City initiative – a major cultural and environmental festival across the city. Two civil society respondents note that the influence of the local media is very high: 'There are five daily newspapers that report on civic engagement and promote activities' and 'The influence of the media on local politics is very high and the media shape public opinion.'

Hanover, Germany

Hanover markets itself as a 'city of gardens', which suggests a confidence in the local authority about promoting the city in this way. The local authority has 'networked services' in terms of cooperation between the directorates of social affairs, culture and planning. The Action Programme for Urban Development also reflects a cross-cutting approach in that it states that integration and equal opportunities are special cross-cutting issues. Sustainable development is identified with the city's political agenda – through the commitment of the leading politicians in the main parties – the Social Democratic Party of Germany (SPD) and the Green party. According to a leading politician: 'Sustainable development is a cross-cutting topic across all council committees; there is no single committee responsible for it.' The Division of Special Planning Issues in the Planning Directorate provides further education on sustainable development issues through seminars and training courses, and also through projects – for example, through the development of the model district Kronsberg.

LA21 has been in existence since 1995 and was initiated by the local authority. However, like Munich, this is seen as being in competition with other programmes (such as the City Development Programme), which have more resources. The local authority has developed a range of approaches for raising awareness in civil society of sustainability issues – publicizing its activities and setting up a community foundation to fund projects on culture and citizen engagement. This was the first German community foundation, set up in 1997, and it funds the area of youth, arts and welfare; according to the fieldworker, it 'sees itself as a catalyst for civic engagement'.

The main interest organizations with which the local authority has links are the media and the construction industry. Both local government and civil society respondents concur on the importance of political continuity and commitment for progress with sustainable development. Moreover, there seems to be support from civil society for the local authority approach to sustainability; one interviewee thought the 'social culture' (in the local authority) one that is open to innovation, was a positive aspect.

Dunkerque Urban Community, France

The local authority has a strategy for sustainable development in which it highlights the need to change attitudes. This strategy is set out in the Sustainable Development Methodology developed by the local authority, which links into training on sustainability. This focus on training reflects the high priority, in general, given to raising awareness in officers and politicians. The local government respondents also note the importance of having well-motivated and committed officers. The key area indicating links between civil society organizations is that of cooperation between industry and the local authority on managing risk. In addition, the fieldworker notes that the development of the sustainable development methodology involved setting up a 'multi-stakeholder' working group (the organizations participating in this were nominated by the local authority). The development of the methodology involved highlighting the sustainable development concerns for these organizations and working on raising awareness on these issues.

Haarlem, The Netherlands

The existence of institutional capacity is indicated through a number of different aspects in the interviews. The mayor is a driving force for sustainability, and there are five vice-mayors working on sustainability issues, which suggests a high level of political commitment in this area. There is also a large budget for training officers and politicians on sustainability issues, and the local authority has set up a Programme Development Department to coordinate all of the departmental work on sustainability. Officers are noted to be highly qualified, related to the high level of training available.

In terms of links to civil society organizations, the local authority seems to be well regarded by citizens, in general; although the overall level of social capacity seems to be fairly low, with one organization commenting that only big institutions are taken account of in terms of affecting policy processes. Both civil society and local government respondents comment on their concerns that the local authority is not sufficiently addressing the bigger issues that face Haarlem (such as climate change).

Ottignies-Louvain la Neuve, Belgium

The situation for the local authority is somewhat unusual in Ottignies-Louvain la Neuve. This, like a number of the other cases, is a university town. However, here the university has considerable municipal power in terms of owning most of the land and providing a large proportion of the local authority budget. This clearly has implications for the capacity of the local authority to act in support of sustainable development. However, the interview responses do indicate that there is political will to progress with sustainable development in the form of a proactive mayor and the integration of these principles within the structure of the organization. This 'mainstreaming' has occurred, in particular, through the appointment of two heads of department from human resources (linking into the 'total quality' management approach adopted by the local authority) and from social services (this person is explicitly responsible for sustainability implementation). The local authority seems to be engaging with a wide range of organizations in civil society. For instance, a representative of the university notes that there is:

> ...a flow of information with the local authority: we have daily contacts with the local authority in relation to the city university and on sustainable development through the meetings of the Commission on Sustainable Development taking place in the municipality.

The interviews suggest some agreement between the local authority and civil society interests on the importance of high-level political will, although there is also a concern that more actions should be implemented.

TOP FIVE CASE STUDIES IN SOUTHERN EUROPE

Calvià, Spain

The interview responses highlight a number of areas of institutional capacity in the sustainability arena. The 'culture' of mainstreaming sustainable development is cited by officers as being very strong and 'embedded' (and appears to remain so despite the change in political complexion). There is strong collaboration between departments on cross-departmental issues and on specific projects, and the team of officers responsible for sustainable development has a high level of expertise. One comment is that:

> …in Calvià, we were characterized by the fact that we had a team composed of staff with both a political and technical background which was very much linked and with a strong cohesion. There was not such a strong differentiation between political and technical staff. There were great inter-exchanges.

There has been strong political commitment to sustainability from the former mayor (whose party was in power for 20 years until the 2003 elections), and the local authority has been driving both the political process and the implementation of policies (as described in Chapter 3). This approach is described by a senior officer as 'interventionist' or even 'paternalist':

> We've seen that the local authority was the driving force of pro-position and implementation. The local authority has done 90 per cent of the work – we've proposed the agenda, the action plan; we've implemented it (local authority respondent).

The fieldworker report notes that, being situated on an island, Calvià may have a stronger identity, and it is possible that a high level of social capacity may be one element of this. A number of sectors of civil society are involved in the LA21 process and in delivering and promoting actions, particularly the hotel industry and the local media. The fieldworker's perspective is that civil society, in general, is informed about proposed actions, but that key sectors are more fully involved. The Calvià Way initiative is one example of capacity-building through specific and visible actions. As noted in Chapter 3, this is linking neighbourhoods and involving different sectors, such as the hotel industry, in incorporating environmental ideas. The local authority has employed a range of approaches to inform citizens and to raise awareness about what individuals can do to become more sustainable. These include forums; newsletters; internet campaigns; media promotions; videos in schools and other public institutions; and 'door-to-door' workers explaining about composting and other domestic initiatives. LA21 is seen by both officers and civil society respondents as an important part of building capacity and knowledge creation, 'enabling' people to understand the links between individual actions and the wider impact. Both sets of respondents have similar views on the nature and level of progress for sustainability, and on the importance of communicating ideas to civil society. A representative of the hotel industry comments: 'What I can say is that there is a will, there is communication, there is an understanding so that people work together and implement the plans and ideas developed together. This is the strong point.'

Ferrara, Italy

Several departments are involved in achieving the local authority's sustainability objectives, and the local authority has a 'formation' and 'information' course for officers to learn how to translate sustainability issues into their areas of work. There is political commitment at a high level, and positive changes have taken place in the working culture of the administration. The comments by local government interviewees suggest that the concept and language of sustainability is being 'embedded' within the local authority: 'Many times people do not even realize that they are doing activities linked to sustainability and this means... that some of the sustainability thematics have been taken in by people and translated into many small initiatives.' It is also noted that: 'We have started a process that it will not be easy to stop since it has reached so many people and departments also within the municipality.'

The main civil society sector that appears to be involved in, and to influence, the sustainability process is business. The media seems to have a local role, although comments are made that it could play a more positive and high-profile role. The fieldworker's perspective is that there is high, but fragmented, civil society involvement in local processes for sustainability. In terms of capacity-building, there are a number of examples cited in the interviews, such as the opening of an 'eco-desk' for citizens to find information on the LA21 process and on specific actions that they can take in areas such as energy efficiency.

Modena Province, Italy

The province of Modena was a pioneer of LA21 in Italy, and its *LA21 Action Plan* and *LA21 Operational Action Plan* (Piano di Azione di Indirizzo Agenda 21, 1999; Piano di Azione Operativo Agenda 21, 2000) are used to mainstream sustainable development in the local authority through diffusing knowledge to departments. The operational plan has also committed the local authority to mainstreaming sustainability criteria and objectives within departmental budgets. The environment department is responsible for carrying the sustainable development work forward; however, managers of all departments are expected to work together on these issues: with the planning department for Environmental Management and Audit Scheme (EMAS) implementation in the industrial district; with the tourism department for introducing environmental impact evaluations before providing incentives for tourism projects; with social services department for linking LA21 *Operational Action Plan* objectives and the *Provincial Health Plan* (Piano Per la Salute, 2002) with the purchasing department in introducing Green Procurement initiatives; and with the accountability department for introducing environmental accountability. Training is provided on specific aspects of sustainability. For instance, a course is being run by the environmental department on eco-building, bringing in architects and university experts to raise awareness in the local authority. In terms of social capacity, there is a high number of NGOs, mainly from the environmental sector, and they are particularly active in the LA21 Forum.

In the business sector, the Associazione Piccole e Medie Imprese (API) (the organization that represents small- and medium-sized enterprises, or SMEs) has introduced sustainable development issues into workshops for businesses, and it has set up an energy consortium offering advice to businesses on how to maximize energy use and save energy. The Federconsumatori (consumers' association) is responsible for collaborating with other organizations, such as schools and NGOs, on environmental projects. According to some respondents, civic engagement is generally very high, with many cultural, political and volunteering organizations; however, it is not clear to what extent these organizations are formally involved in the sustainable development policy process. There are formal agreements on partnership for implementing projects and informal relations to discuss, promote and monitor progress during workshops, the LA21 forum and bilateral meetings with local officers. A multi-media CD has been created, demonstrating partnerships projects on sustainable development that have already been implemented at the provincial level. A permanent on-line Provincial Observatory on Sustainable Development collects and provides good examples and initiatives/projects for local sustainability promoted by different local authorities, civil society organizations and citizens.

The perception is that there is a good relationship between different groups in the public and private sector, and, aside from capacity-building through the LA21 forum, the local authority works with a range of organizations. It has an agreement through the business organizations to support SMEs that take eco-certification, and the environmental department has developed links with the consumers' association and the producers of heating systems, with the aim of promoting the installation of energy-efficient systems at affordable prices. This department also has links with other public-sector organizations, health agencies, cultural associations and environmental NGOs, and seeks their input into developing solutions to sustainability issues.

Santa Perpetua de Mogoda, Spain

The interviews have highlighted the existence of political will and commitment, with the mayor leading the process (as with Barcelona, the Green communists are in power and have been for 25 years). The mainstreaming of sustainability principles within all departments, through LA21, is noted and the LA21 officer is cited as being central to the process. The main sectors currently engaged in the LA21 process are industry and the university, and interviewees from these sectors (perhaps not surprisingly) saw LA21 as a 'meaningful' process. In terms of capacity-building, it is commented that 'trust' in the LA21 person, both from the local authority and from traditionally 'excluded' groups, such as farmers, has had a beneficial impact upon the 'dialogue' between these sectors. The local authority has also created an environment commission as a point of contact for civil society organizations; however, respondents are not clear about the role and impact of this commission. Both sets of respondents have a similar perspective on the ways in which culture is changing within the local authority, and it is felt that LA21 has had a positive influence here.

Barcelona Province, Spain

The key points cited in the interviews are the existence of professional and technical expertise for sustainable development, at the provincial level permitting, for example, the pioneering ideas on Green purchasing, and the political commitment of the mayor and other politicians (suggested to be linked to the fact that the Green communists are in power). The approach of developing and disseminating the LA21 model to local authorities in the region is perceived as beneficial through the technical support and financial assistance provided.

A senior officer notes that 100 local authorities have started to 'walk towards environmental sustainability'; however, an expansion of this model of sustainable development requires 'changes in mentalities and ways of acting that ask for efforts'; local authorities 'have to stop thinking about processes and definitions and to go for action'. Moreover, it is commented that:

> The LA21 is a change in the way of thinking of the local authorities because it asks to plan in the long term and it asks for mainstreaming and... for citizens' participation. All these concepts and ideas are very new and, sometimes the local authorities are a little bit reluctant to lose power and control.

In terms of capacity-building, the role of the provincial level in developing policies for sustainable development is seen as important. A representative of the political opposition notes:

> Twenty years ago it was impossible to think that the municipalities would meet in a network like the network of cities and towns towards sustainability. The [province] has helped... the municipalities [a lot] that had initiatives; it has provided them with the resources to study models from other countries and it has given them technical advice.

TOP FOUR CASE STUDIES IN NORTHERN EUROPE

Gotland, Sweden

As noted in Chapter 3, the island of Gotland is an 'eco-municipality', and there is an 'eco-team' within the local authority. In terms of institutional capacity, the interviewees cite the importance of political will and political consensus in Gotland becoming an eco-municipality. The role of individuals is also noted, in particular the 'keyholder's spider-web connections' to other individuals within the local authority, and to civil society. There are links between civil society and the local policy process, specifically through individuals working in both civil society organizations, such as the tourist office or educational institutions, and being politically active on local government boards and committees (a common practice in Sweden). Both the local government and civil society responses show a strong consensus on where progress has been made, and on the important context of being an island and an 'eco-municipality'. In terms of capacity-building, LA21 seems to be well integrated within the communication links set up by the local authority, and 'trust' in the key individuals, as well as in local government as an institution, appears to be an important factor.

Albertslund, Denmark

In Albertslund the perception is that there is 'mainstreaming' of sustainability in that an environmental group exists, consisting of all departments, whose remit is to implement EMAS; cross-departmental working is also operating, in general. The local authority regularly holds discussions in which the environment department answers questions that other departments raise on sustainable development issues. Another important aspect is political commitment to sustainable development, and a confidence within the local authority that it is making progress. The LA21 process is seen as being successful, partly due to the way the process has developed. LA21 was originally started by the inhabitants, but was then supported by the local authority. An active LA21 centre operates, and small citizens' groups are represented by a bigger citizens' group on the Agenda 21 Centre Board. This is perceived by interviewees to aid cooperation between local government and civil society. The Green Award initiative by the local authority, given to individual citizens for achievements in the arena of sustainability, is also noted as important in the relationship between local government and civil society.

Stavanger, Norway

The key factors in Stavanger are the political will behind the development and implementation of sustainability policies and the 'mainstreaming' of sustainability within local government working practices and areas, such as purchasing policy. This commitment at a high level is noted by both local government and civil society organizations. Several sectors in civil society are engaged in the policy process. In particular, environmental NGOs are perceived to have a strong role (through LA21), as well as business (through the Green City initiative set up by the local authority) and citizens' groups (through LA21 and the Greenday citizens' organization, again created by the local authority). The local media is also seen as having a role in spreading information about sustainability issues. On the issue of links between the local authority and civil society organizations, according to one senior officer: 'I think that the networks, the common networks, are very important for the environmental and sustainable development work.'

In terms of capacity-building measures, the interviews note the existence of a website for individuals in the city to measure their ecological footprint, and the involvement of groups in the initiatives described above.

Tampere, Finland

The main positive factors for institutional capacity are the continuity of key officers – the sustainability coordinator has been in post for several years – and the willingness of decision-makers to be innovative in implementing sustainable development. This is also linked to the high level of knowledge that exists within the local authority. Sustainability principles are part of the local authority strategies and are also integrated within all levels of the administration. The decision to become a member of Eurocities suggests a recognition by the local authority of the relevance of international networks to support its work.

In terms of civil society interests, the main links appear to be with the university and with business. Other sectors are active, but this seems to be almost *despite* the local authority's decision not to use the suggested LA21 programme (developed with civil society organizations). The perception is that this decision has caused strains in the relationship between the local authority and some sectors of civil society.

CONCLUSIONS

The empirical material on the 'processes' of government and governance for sustainability shows that many of the local authorities are getting to grips with developing and strengthening institutional capacity, particularly through the mainstreaming of sustainability principles within policy structures and processes, and the training and education of officers and politicians on sustainable development issues. A (small) number of key interest organizations are actively involved in the sustainable development processes in the case studies, and in some cases an active civil society, in terms of volunteering and political engagement, is also evident. Capacity-building initiatives are being developed for improving the knowledge, awareness and engagement of both civil society, more generally, and organizations, and LA21 is clearly an important tool in this area. In terms of the relevant Aalborg Principles and Commitments, there clearly has been a positive shift towards developing 'local strategies towards sustainability', and involving key sectors of civil society. However, the 'participation' and engagement of citizens in the decision-making process is less evident. Chapter 5 discusses these issues in more depth by analysing the broader trends and processes of capacity and capacity-building for sustainable development.

Local Government and Civil Society

INTRODUCTION

The term 'governance' implies that a framework and procedures are in place for cooperation between local government and civil society. Following on from the analysis of the empirical material in the 40 case studies, this chapter moves to a broader analysis of the themes and trends in terms of the relations between civil society interests and local government, and the nature of institutional capacity within local authorities. The rich source of material from the questionnaire responses forms the basis for this analysis, although in the latter part of this chapter further interpretation of the interview data is used to consider the nature and extent of capacity-building in the 40 case studies.

Where appropriate, the data are again divided according to the four 'regions' devised for the research. The primary purpose here is to consider whether governance and government for sustainable development is more likely to be realized in municipalities where there are stronger links between civil society and local government. The analysis begins by examining the broad perspectives of respondents on the nature of 'sustainable development'.

UNDERSTANDING THE CONCEPT OF SUSTAINABLE DEVELOPMENT

Understandably, there is a great diversity in the 1075 respondents in conceptualizing 'sustainable development'. Generally, the concept seems to be better known in local authorities than in civil society and is generally less known in Eastern European cases (as, indeed, both the fieldworker summary reports and the interviews suggest). As Table 5.1 shows, there is a high proportion of unclassifiable answers (28 per cent), a strong dominance of environmental thinking in the Northern and Southern European case studies, and a variety of perspectives in the Western and Eastern European case studies (although these mainly relate to the integration of the social, economic and environmental dimensions, or the future use of resources).

Table 5.1 *Understanding the concept of sustainable development (per cent)*

Classification of open answers	Northern Europe	Southern Europe	Western Europe	Eastern Europe	All cases
Social, economic and environmental	13	16	23	27	21
Social or economic, with or without mentioning the environment	10	22	11	19	16
Using resources sparingly for future generations	25	15	15	12	16
Environment	32	23	13	11	19
Unclassified	19	24	38	30	28
Total %	**100**	**100**	**100**	**100**	**100**

RELATIVE IMPORTANCE OF LOCAL GOVERNMENT DEPARTMENTS

In all four regions, respondents see the economic, planning and environmental departments as more central to sustainability policies than the departments for social/welfare or health. This tendency is stronger in Northern and Eastern European case studies than those in Southern and Western Europe, where the social/welfare departments are given a high priority by the respondents. The central role played by the local planning departments is evident in most case studies, the exceptions being those in Eastern Europe where economic development features more strongly. The importance of the environmental departments was most strongly underlined in Southern and Western European cases.

ROLE OF GOVERNMENT AND CIVIL SOCIETY IN RAISING AWARENESS OF SUSTAINABILITY

The role of national and sub-national institutions is not a principal focus of this study; however, it may be reasonable to conclude from the research that once a country has legislated about a strategy for development, local governments, non-governmental organizations (NGOs) and civil society interests may be more likely to become engaged in working towards national goals. When asked about

Table 5.2 Regional classification of importance of local government departments (percentage of 'yes' answers in total sample)

Northern Europe	Southern Europe	Western Europe	Eastern Europe	All cases
Planning (50)	Planning (61)	Planning (63)	Economic (49)	Planning (53)
Economic (48)	Environment (51)	Economic (51)	Planning (34)	Economic (48)
Environment (24)	Economic (43)	Environment (46)	Environment (26)	Environment (38)
Social/welfare (9)	Social/welfare (35)	Social/welfare (39)	Social/welfare (25)	Social/welfare (28)
Health (4)	Health (14)	Health (15)	Health (7)	Health (10)

the importance of national and sub-national authorities in raising awareness and providing training on sustainable development, 29 per cent responded positively in the Western European case studies, 23 per cent in Southern Europe, 18 per cent in Northern Europe and 10 per cent in Eastern Europe. Local government is identified in most of the case studies as having the main responsibility for awareness-raising measures for sustainable development, and this is particularly so in the Eastern European cases. NGOs are also seen by most as important in this area of governance, and the influence of a combination of local government, sub-national and national government, and NGOs is strongly visible in the Western European case studies. This could suggest that modes of cooperation between local government and civil society organizations are generally more developed in these towns and cities. In addition, the role of international NGOs in this arena reinforces the notion that sustainable development should be a process that brings the global and international scenario into local societies.

Looking in more depth, respondents in Northern European case studies have received training on sustainability issues to a higher extent and through more diverse channels than others. This is true for general awareness-raising, specific courses, seminars and briefings, workshops and forums, and the internet (and for local authorities, the intranet). In Southern European case studies, the emphasis is on training through conferences, seminars and public lectures. For those in Western Europe, the focus is on general awareness-raising and the intranet, and for Eastern European respondents the media has been a more important channel for training and awareness-raising than for respondents in the other regions.

'PARTNERSHIPS' BETWEEN LOCAL GOVERNMENT AND CIVIL SOCIETY

'Partnerships' between local government and civil society interests have come to be seen as common forms to implement bottom-up processes of local government.

In all regions a majority of the respondents say that it is important to develop and maintain partnerships between local government and civil society. The support for partnerships is significantly stronger in Southern European cases than elsewhere and reinforces the findings in Table 5.3 about the activity level of civil society, in general.

The difference in the importance attached to 'partnerships' by civil society organizations and local governments is only slight, although civil society respondents are more positive. There are no significant differences between cases by 'region' with regard to the evaluation of how actively the local governments have acted in order to improve relations with civil society. The material, nevertheless, points to some contrasts between the opinions of local authorities and civil society organizations, especially in Western and Eastern European case studies. For example, local government representatives may think that they have improved internal local relationships, while representatives of civil society are less enthusiastic. Table 5.4 presents responses to the question: 'Is your local

Table 5.3 *Support for local 'partnerships' among local authority and civil society respondents (averages, based on scale 0–3 with 0 = no extent and 3 = very high extent)*

	All	Local government	Civil society	Difference
Eastern Europe	2.4	2.3	2.4	0.1
Western Europe	2.4	2.5	2.4	0.1
Southern Europe	2.6	2.6	2.6	0.0
Northern Europe	2.5	2.4	2.6	0.2

authority supportive of initiatives and tools that enhance relationships between local government and civil society organizations?'

Tables 5.3 and 5.4 relate to two important governance aspects: the relevance and importance that both local governments and civil society organizations

Table 5.4 *Support for local government initiatives and tools to enhance relationships with civil society organizations (averages, based on scale 0–3 with 0 = no extent and 3 = very high extent)*

	All	Local government	Civil society	Difference
Eastern Europe	1.8	2.0	1.7	0.3
Western Europe	1.9	1.2	1.7	0.5
Southern Europe	1.8	1.8	1.7	0.1
Northern Europe	1.8	1.9	1.6	0.3

attach to the development and nurturing of 'partnerships' between these sectors, and general confidence within civil society organizations that local governments will implement cooperative forms of governing. Civil society organizations tend to stress the necessity of relationships (formal and informal) more than local governments, while the latter tend to think more highly of their own measures taken to implement cooperative forms of decision-making.

Tables 5.5 and 5.6 present the ten cases with the highest 'averages' for all respondents in terms of the perceived importance of developing and maintaining partnerships (Table 5.5), and of the perceived support by the local authority of tools and initiatives to enhance these relationships (Table 5.6).

Several of these case studies are in the top 20 examples for sustainable development progress and the top 18 for institutional/social capacity and capacity building in Chapters 3 to 4 – namely, Barcelona, Santa Perpetua de Mogoda, Calvià, Ferrara and Tampere. However, five of those which are not included in these groups are also represented here (Baia Mare, Beja, Stirling, Dungannon and South Tyrone, and Falkenberg). These findings may reflect the point that

Table 5.5 *Importance of 'partnerships' (averages based on scale 0–3 with 0 = no extent and 3 = very high extent)*

	Average
1 Barcelona Province, Spain	2.8
2 Baia Mare, Romania	2.8
3 Beja, Portugal	2.8
4 Stirling, UK	2.7
5 Santa Perpetua de Mogoda, Spain	2.7
6 Dungannon and South Tyrone, Northern Ireland, UK	2.7
7 Calvià, Spain	2.7
8 Ferrara, Italy	2.7
9 Tampere, Finland	2.7
10 Falkenberg, Sweden	2.6

the existence of partnerships can actually mean little in practice. Moreover, the influence of partnerships depends upon which interests are involved, the relative power and resources of these groups and organizations, and the importance placed on developing relationships for sustainable development, both by local government and interest organizations. It may also be the case that improvement of relations between local governments and civil society is occurring, but that the results for sustainable development are less visible.

Table 5.6 *Extent that local authority is supportive of tools and initiatives to enhance relationships (averages based on scale 0–3 with 0 = no extent and 3 = very high extent)*

	Average
1 Stirling, UK	2.4
2 Baia Mare, Romania	2.3
3 Ferrara, Italy	2.1
4 Valenciennes, France	2.1
5 Falkenberg, Sweden	2.1
6 Santa Perpetua de Mogoda, Spain	2.1
7 Stavanger, Norway	2.1
8 Celle Ligure, Italy	2.0
9 Växjö, Sweden	2.0
10 Veliko Turnovo, Bulgaria	2.0

Case studies that rate highly in both tables are Baia Mare, Stirling, Ferrara, Santa Perpetua de Mogoda and Falkenberg. Those case studies where respondents highly value partnerships but do not think that their local authority is supportive of enhancing these relationships are Barcelona, Calvià, Beja, Dungannon and South Tyrone, and Tampere.

The starting point for establishing active partnerships varies between the case studies, and there are also distinctions between the aggregate responses for the four regions, especially with regard to the relative impact of environmental NGOs, religious groups and ethnic minorities (see Table 5.7). In Northern European case studies, those respondents who emphasize the role of environmental NGOs over other groups give little attention to the role of religious and ethnic minority groups. Respondents in all four regions perceive business organizations as playing an important role in decision-making processes.

The role of religious organizations emerges mainly in some of the East European case studies, and the data show that ethnic minority groups are perceived as more important both in Western and Eastern European case studies than those in Southern Europe. In comparison to the strong differences by region in the role of environmental, religious and ethnic minority groups, there is little distinction between the regions in terms of the impact of political parties and social NGOs. Respondents in Northern European case studies express the influence of political parties and tend to neglect social NGOs more than respondents from the other case studies. Table 5.7 verifies that political parties in the majority of cases are considered to be the most important channel for civil society influence on sustainable development, and the legitimacy of political parties and environmental NGOs is higher among Northern European case studies than elsewhere. It is also interesting to note that business organizations and environmental NGOs rate much higher among all respondents than do social NGOs, religious groups and ethnic minority groups. Of the other categories in this question, very few respondents saw youth and childrens' organizations or women's groups as influential. The evidence, therefore, suggests that sustainable development needs political will, support of local business and respect for nature values.

THE RESPONSIBILITY OF LOCAL GOVERNMENTS

The data clearly show that it is local government who is expected to take responsibility for the mainstreaming of sustainable development and the implementation of policies to reflect this. This is substantiated by responses on the balance of influence between local governments and civil societies. In case studies across all four regions, responses to the question 'Does your organization have an influence on the sustainable development policy process in your locality?' show (perhaps not surprisingly) that local government respondents perceive themselves as having greater influence over the local sustainability process than do civil society representatives (see Table 5.8). The gap between these estimations is smallest in Eastern European case studies where both categories express high self-confidence. While there is little reason to doubt that local authority officers and politicians are those with most power over local affairs, the varying influence of different civil society groups is clearly a more complex issue to assess.

The central role played by local governments is substantiated by local authority officers themselves and by the opinions of respondents, generally. In

Table 5.7 *Evaluations of influence from different civil society organizations/groups on sustainable development processes (percentage of responses combined in categories 'a little extent', 'a high extent' and 'a very high extent')*

Northern Europe (%)	Southern Europe (%)	Western Europe (%)	Eastern Europe (%)	All cases
Political (81)	Political (68)	Political (72)	Political (64)	Political (70)
Environmental (70)	Business (55)	Environmental (57)	Business (55)	Environmental (55)
Business (47)	Environmental (50)	Business (49)	Environmental (48)	Business (52)
Social (25)	Social (30)	Social (40)	Social (41)	Social (35)
Religious (2)	Religious (9)	Religious (11)	Religious (20)	Religious (11)
Ethnic (1)	Ethnic (2)	Ethnic (9)	Ethnic (8)	Ethnic (5)

Table 5.8 *Estimate of own organization's influence on local sustainable development policies (averages based on scale 0–3 with 0 = no extent and 3 = very high extent)*

	Local government	Civil society	Difference
Eastern Europe	2.2	1.8	0.4
Western Europe	1.9	1.3	0.6
Southern Europe	1.9	1.4	0.5
Northern Europe	2.1	1.5	0.6

all four regions a majority of respondents represent local government and, of these, three out of four answers confirm that their organization influences local processes for sustainability. Generally speaking, local sustainability expertise tends to rest with the officers in local authorities. Civil society representatives in Northern European case studies are most convinced of their own influence, closely followed by those in Southern European case studies. In Western European case studies, civil society respondents are less convinced about their influence than those in Northern and Southern Europe, but are still much more confident on this issue than those in Eastern Europe.

The evidence shows that local government respondents consider their own organizational influence on decisions concerning sustainable development as central. The ten local governments and civil societies with the highest sense of their organization influencing policies are shown in Table 5.9.

A comparison of case studies appearing in both columns of Table 5.9 shows only a few appearing in both lists, which suggest divergent views between local government and civil society organizations regarding the level of influence that each has. Case studies where our data suggest that the sense of influence may be higher in civil society than among the local governments are Modena Province, South-west Finland Agenda, Lahti, Vantaa, Falkenberg, Barcelona Province, Stirling and Dunajska Luzna.

The high level of satisfaction that local government respondents have about their own organizational influence is not always supported by opinions in civil society. One factor here may be the confidence or 'trust' that civil society interests have in their local authority, but also in local government per se in terms of its powers and political commitment to act in support of sustainable development. The questionnaire asks respondents to comment on three related aspects:

1   the extent to which leading politicians are committed to addressing sustainable development issues;
2   the extent to which the local authority has a long-term vision for sustainability;
3   how well developed the strategy for sustainability is.

Table 5.10 shows the aggregate data for the responses to all three questions.

Table 5.9 *Ten case studies with organizations showing highest sense of influencing sustainable development Policies (averages based on scale 0–3 with 0 = no extent and 3 = very high extent)*

Local government		Civil society	
1 Celle Ligure, Italy	2.2	1 Modena Province, Italy	1.5
2 Durham County Council, UK	2.1	2 South-west Finland Agenda, Finland	1.5
3 Växjö, Sweden	2.1	3 Celle Ligure, Italy	1.4
4 Redbridge, UK	2.0	4 Durham County Council, UK	1.4
5 Tampere, Finland	2.0	5 Lahti, Finland	1.4
6 Calvià, Spain	2.0	6 Dunajska Luzna, Slovakia	1.4
7 Santa Perpetua de Mogoda, Spain	1.9	7 Ferrara, Italy	1.3
8 Orastie, Romania	1.8	8 Falkenberg, Sweden	1.3
9 Ferrara, Italy	1.8	9 Stirling, UK	1.3
10 Gdansk, Poland	1.8	10 Vantaa, Finland	1.3
11 Dubrovnik, Croatia	1.8	11 Barcelona Province, Spain	1.3
12 Stavanger, Norway	1.8		
All local government	1.6	All civil society	1.0

Table 5.10 *Confidence in local government approach to sustainability policy-making (averages based on scale 0–3 with 0 = no extent and 3 = very high extent)*

	All	Local government	Civil society	Difference
Eastern Europe	1.7	1.8	1.5	0.3
Western Europe	1.8	2.0	1.6	0.4
Southern Europe	1.5	1.6	1.4	0.2
Northern Europe	1.7	1.7	1.7	0.0
All cases	1.7	1.8	1.5	0.3

The general level of confidence in the policies of local governments is higher than the average value in Western European case studies (both in local governments and in civil society organizations) and relatively low in those in Southern Europe. In Western European case studies local government respondents tend to think more highly of their own policy capacity than do respondents from civil society organizations. In Northern European case studies civil society and local government respondents have confidence on an equal level, which may reflect a more consensus-style type of politics, or may simply reflect a relatively high proportion of politicians among these local government respondents. Table 5.11 shows those cases where confidence by all respondents in the policy-making ability of local government is strongest.

A number of the case studies in Table 5.11 correlate with those identified in Chapters 3 and 4 as being more advanced in policy outcomes and in terms of their capacity for sustainable development: Calvià, Tampere, Hanover, Albertslund, Munich and Dunajska Luzna all received ratings of achieving

Table 5.11 *Cases showing highest level of confidence in local government policy-making capacity (averages based on scale 0–3 with 0 = no confidence and 3 = very high level of confidence, ranking order)*

	Average
1 Calvià, Spain	2.2
2 Tampere, Finland	2.1
3 Albertslund, Denmark	2.1
4 Baia Mare, Romania	2.0
5 Valenciennes, France	2.0
6 Hanover, Germany	2.0
7 Munich, Germany	1.9
8 Vantaa, Finland	1.9
9 Durham County Council, UK	1.9
10 London Borough of Redbridge, UK	1.9
11 Dunajska Luzna, Slovakia	1.9

considerable progress. However, Baia Mare, Valenciennes, Durham County Council, Redbridge and Vantaa also have high rankings in Table 5.11.

In order to make some judgement about the extent of civil society activity and engagement, more generally, respondents were asked to comment on the level of activity of civil society in their municipality (but not specifically in relation to sustainable development). The results are presented separately for respondents from local government and civil society.

In eight of these cases (Dunajska Luzna, Baia Mare, Albertslund, Celle Ligure, Modena Province, Ferrara, Granollers and Barcelona Province) respondents from the local authority and civil society organizations perceive there is an active civil society, thus placing these among the top ten in both columns of Table 5.12. Valenciennes and Munich are cases where representatives of local government think that they have a more active civil society than the civil society responses indicate. Contrastingly, Santa Perpetua de Mogoda, Ottignies-Louvain la Neuve and Dungannon and South Tyrone are case studies with highly active civil societies in the opinions of the civil society organizations, but not by their local government respondents.

EXPERIENCE OF JOINT SUSTAINABILITY PROJECTS BETWEEN LOCAL GOVERNMENTS AND CIVIL SOCIETY ORGANIZATIONS

The respondents were asked to what extent their organization had been engaged in a joint project to develop skills, knowledge and awareness during the last three years. Table 5.13 shows that a clear majority of all respondents had been involved in joint projects. However, this was more common among respondents from local governments, NGOs, and especially among semi-governmental professions, than among those representing business or other civil society organizations. In some of the case studies (Dungannon and South Tyrone, Ottignies-Louvain la Neuve, Modena Province and Tampere) all respondents had represented an organization in joint projects between organizations. Seven of the ten 'reference' case studies belong to the group with comparatively little experience of joint projects between organizations. However, 'reference' case studies, which do rank higher in this respect, are Beja, Haarlem and, especially, Ottignies-Louvain la Neuve.

The highest experience of joint projects for sustainability derives from contacts between local environment departments and environmental NGOs. Experiences of organizational cooperation with social welfare departments, social NGOs or business are reported as fairly rare, although these are still more common than organizational cooperation with political parties, women's groups, ethnic minority groups or religious groups. Respondents representing local government have the most varied experience of joint projects with all kinds of organizations, especially with regards to the economic department, business organizations and political parties.

Table 5.12 *Case studies with highest level of civil society activity (averages based on scale 0–3 with 0 = no extent and 3 = very high extent)*

Local government	Average	Civil society	Average
1 Dunajska Luzna, Slovakia	2.2	1 Dunajska Luzna, Slovakia	2.2
2 Valenciennes, France	2.1	2 Baia Mare, Romania	2.1
3 Albertslund, Denmark	2.0	3 Modena Province, Italy	2.1
4 Celle Ligure, Italy	2.0	4 Ferrara, Italy	1.9
5 Modena Province, Italy	2.0	5 Albertslund, Denmark	1.9
6 Ferrara, Italy	1.9	6 Santa Perpetua de Mogoda, Spain	1.8
7 Granollers, Spain	1.9	7 Granollers, Spain	1.8
8 Munich, Germany	1.9	8 Ottignies-Louvain la Neuve, Belgium	1.8
9 Baia Mare, Romania	1.8	9 Barcelona Province, Spain	1.8
10 Barcelona Province, Spain	1.8	10 Dungannon and South Tyrone, UK	1.8

Table 5.13 *Reported activity in local organizational joint projects during 2000–2003 (percentage of respondents reporting on cooperation between their own and at least one other organization)*

<79.9%	80–89.9%	90–99.9%	Very high (100%)
Anyksciai, Lithuania	Albertslund, Denmark	Baia Mare, Romania	Dungannon and South Tyrone, UK
Dubrovnik, Croatia	Beja, Portugal	Celle Ligure, Italy	Ottignies-Louvain la Neuve, Belgium
Dunajska Luzna, Slovakia	Calvià, Spain	Barcelona Province, Spain	Modena Province, Italy
Fano, Italy	Dunkerque Urban Community, France	Durham County Council, UK	Tampere, Finland
Frederikshavn, Denmark	Falkenberg, Sweden	Ferrara, Italy	
Gotland , Sweden	Gdansk, Poland	Korolev, Russia	
Granollers, France	Haarlem, The Netherlands	Munich, Germany	
Kuressaare, Estonia	Hanover, Germany	London Borough of Redbridge, UK	
Orastie, Romania	Lahti, Finland	Santa Perpetua de Mogoda, Spain	
Tallinn, Estonia	Valenciennes, France	Stavanger, Norway	
Thessaloniki, Greece	Veliko Turnovo, Bulgaria	Stirling, UK	
Vantaa, Finland		South-west Finland Agenda, Finland	
		Växjö, Sweden	

CONCLUSIONS ON LOCAL GOVERNMENT AND CIVIL SOCIETY RELATIONS

This chapter has highlighted the emerging themes on the nature of governance (the relationship between local government, civil society interests and civil society, in general) and government (the perceptions of both local authorities and civil society interests on the role and influence of local government in the sustainability policy-making arena). Representatives of civil society sectors who appear to be most engaged in the process – universities, business organizations and media representatives, as well as activists in specific NGOs – appear to have considerable knowledge of, and commitment to, local sustainability projects and partnerships. They represent a part of civil society that has most often cooperated with local government on awareness-raising campaigns and other modes of promoting and implementing sustainability, and clearly their engagement at local level is invaluable. Civil society respondents tend to value the idea of 'partnerships' more than local government does, while confidence about the capacity of local government to influence sustainable politics as a rule is stronger inside local authorities than among their corresponding civil respondents.

Irrespective of place, local governments who have a record of commitment to sustainable development and governance processes in place to deliver this – for example, through LA21 or other active measures – tend to be met by higher levels of confidence from civil society with respect to their devotion to sustainable development. Moreover, these local governments tend to be more self-confident about their competence to be proactive on sustainable development than in municipalities without a well-developed sustainability strategy and policies. Political parties are perceived as important collaborators for civil society organizations in many cases, and it is interesting to reiterate the point made in Chapter 4 that some of the most progressive case studies from Southern and Western Europe have developed under a strong 'Red–Green' political leadership.

Chapter 6 explores further the themes emerging from the research on the processes of governing for sustainable development across Europe.

Chapter 6

Governing for Sustainability

INTRODUCTION

This book has so far examined the ways in which local governments and civil society interact in response to the challenges of sustainable development. This chapter draws together the key themes from the previous empirical chapters and provides conclusions on the nature of local governing processes for sustainability. More specifically, in this chapter we draw together the qualitative and quantitative evidence reviewed earlier in order to provide an explanatory model of the relationships that exist in the processes of governing sustainable cities. This is followed by a synthesis of the main themes that have emerged from the research work. We then make suggestions and recommendations for policy action, which is the focus of Chapter 7.

THE DEVELOPING INSTITUTIONAL AND SOCIAL CAPACITIES FOR URBAN SUSTAINABILITY (DISCUS)
RESEARCH QUESTIONS

To recap, the three questions that guided the research work were:

1   What constitutes 'success' in urban sustainable development policy and practice?
2   What are the factors and conditions that permit or obstruct 'success' in local sustainable development policy and practice?
3   What constitutes 'good governance' for urban sustainable development?

As we have seen, defining 'success' in sustainability policy-making and implementation is highly problematic both from a theoretical and a practical point of view. In particular, within the field of sustainable development policy, outcomes are much more difficult to explain than administrative and political procedures. Nevertheless, as suggested in the research questions and in the earlier discussions, we expect there to be a relationship between policy procedures and policy outcomes.

The discussion in Chapter 2 indicated that we expected to find a strong relationship between institutional capacity and social capacity, with local governments playing a key role in influencing the creation of both institutional and social capacity by affecting the mobilization of local-level agents within the sphere of sustainability policies. Thus, the institutional framework of sub-national (local or regional) government could be a crucial factor in determining the long-term prospects for civil society engagement in sustainability policy processes. Our main hypothesis was, thus, that *there are causal links between (good) governance and sustainable development policy success.*

Based on the assumptions in the current academic and policy discourses on 'good governance' and sustainable development, it was possible for us to establish the following working hypothesis:

> The higher the levels of both social and institutional capacity, the greater is the likelihood of sustainable development policy achievements (that is, 'good' governance for sustainable development). Conversely, the lower the levels of social capacity and/or institutional capacity, the greater is the likelihood of sustainable development policy failure.

This relationship is illustrated in Box 6.1.

Box 6.1 *The relationship between social and institutional capacity, capacity-building measures and sustainable development policy outcomes*

Institutional capacity for sustainable development

Social capacity for sustainable development	Higher	Lower
Higher	**1 Dynamic governing** →Active sustainability capacity-building →**High** possibility for sustainability policy outcomes	**4 Voluntary governing** →Voluntary sustainable development capacity-building →**Low** possibility for sustainability policy outcomes
Lower	**2 Active government** Medium sustainable development capacity-building **Medium** or **fairly high** possibility for sustainability policy outcomes	**3 Passive government** →**Low/no** sustainable development capacity-building →Sustainability policy failure

The first category in Box 6.1 (*dynamic governing*) follows our hypothesis about the positive effects of co-governing of local government and civil society agents. The basis for this assumption is, as described earlier, in both the governance and ecological modernization literature. It is also clear that there must be an ongoing, active and planned process of capacity-building for sustainable development, linking civil society and local government.

Our assumption for *active government* is that results can also be achieved if at least the institutional structures – that is, the structures of local governments – have enough capacity for sustainable development. These are *eco-efficient governments* in that they are efficient government with some governance structures in place for delivering sustainable development policies, but are focusing less on development structures and mechanisms for engaging civil society in policy processes.

The third case (*passive government*) would, in practice, mean policy failure for sustainable development policies at the local level. Even in this case local government would retain some routine tasks within the national setting; but local action would be restricted to a minimum. This situation is likely to be stable as there seems to be low pressure from civil society for change as the social capacity for sustainable development is also very low.

Finally, a more problematic case to interpret is the situation where civil society is expected to act alone in order to reach sustainability. This situation would mean some form of *voluntary governing*. The functions of local government are only meant for routine tasks, although there could still be (fairly low) positive outcomes for sustainability. In addition, capacity-building for sustainable development would, in practice, be rather limited and only distributed by and through civil society actors.

In previous chapters we have examined the different elements of this model in detail as they have appeared in the empirical material from 40 case studies. In the following section we present the findings in aggregate form, using the four categories described above to provide the broad trends that emerge regarding local government capacity, civil society capacity, capacity-building, and policy outcomes.

KEY TRENDS FOR SUSTAINABLE DEVELOPMENT PROCESS AND PROGRESS

In order to identify key trends, the first index is created from the scorings allocated to each of the 40 case studies, based on the interview material only. As explained in Chapters 3 and 4, all case studies were given a ranking between *low extent* to *high extent*. *Low extent* was then given a score of 5, *medium extent* a score of 10 and *high extent* a score of 15, although where it was judged that cases fell between these, a mid-way score was allocated (for example, *low-medium* is 7.5). This is presented in Figure 6.1 for sustainable development policy outcomes, capacity in local government and civil society, and capacity-building.

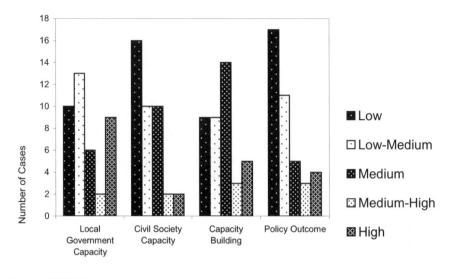

Source: DISCUS database

Figure 6.1 *Rankings from the qualitative material*

The cases are situated within one of the five categories (from low to high) according to their 'local government capacity' and 'civil society capacity'. If we then relate these categories to the four categories of 'governing', this provides the following division of case studies:

- 10 cases (25 per cent) fall in the category of *dynamic governing*
- 19 cases (47.5 per cent) fall in the category of *passive government*
- 7 cases (17.5 per cent) fall in the category of *active government*
- 4 cases (10 per cent) fall in the category of *voluntary governing*.

Figure 6.2 shows that the assumed capacity levels for both local government and civil society organizations (here using a scale of 0–1 for the average values, and thus different from the values used in Chapters 3–5) reflect the rationale behind the four categories. Thus, there are higher overall capacity levels in the group of ten *dynamic* cases; local government capacity is lower for *active* and *passive* governments, but lowest for *voluntary governing*.

In terms of capacity-building, Figure 6.3 suggests that local and regional governments that are either active alone or active in cooperation with civil society also show a clear and visible difference in the number and scope of capacity-building activities conducted within the locality. This pattern is also visible if we consider only the answers to the questionnaire. However, the differences between local government opinions and civil society opinions on the number and level of capacity-building activities are fairly small.

Following our theoretical expectations, it is also assumed that the four types of governing structures should also have differential impacts upon sustainable

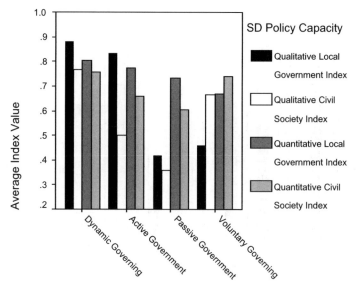

Source: DISCUS database

Figure 6.2 *Governing and capacity*

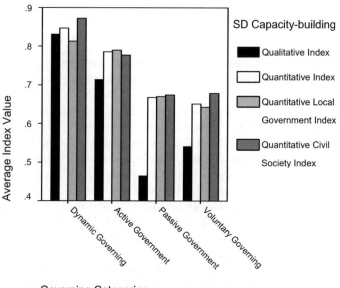

Source: DISCUS database

Figure 6.3 *Governing and capacity-building for sustainable development*

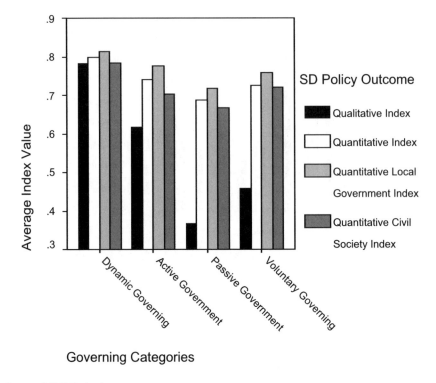

Source: DISCUS database

Figure 6.4 *Governing and sustainable development policy outcomes*

development policy outcomes. As Figure 6.4 shows, the best results are achieved if local and sub-national governments develop relationships with civil society. *Dynamic governing* patterns are clearly most efficient in achieving positive policy achievements in an area where cooperation is essential. Results (but to a lower extent) can also be achieved if local government is *active* in terms of developing its own capacity for delivering sustainable development – but not taking civil society fully into account. *Passive governments*, only carrying out routine tasks, are clearly lagging behind in terms of policy outcomes. Active civil society can, to some extent, help this process; but progress is still marginal. In general, however, the civil society respondents appear more critical than local government with regard to the policy outcomes. The difference in the evaluation levels can partly be explained by the fact that the index is based on general questions on performance related to a selection of items covering environmental, economic and social aspects. Some of these policy areas can, for some countries, be out of reach for local governments, and performance might thus already be guaranteed by national-level actors.

In Figure 6.5, we use only the *survey-based* capacity indexes, measuring the opinions of all the local government officials and civil society representatives in the 40 case studies, in order to show the location of these within the four

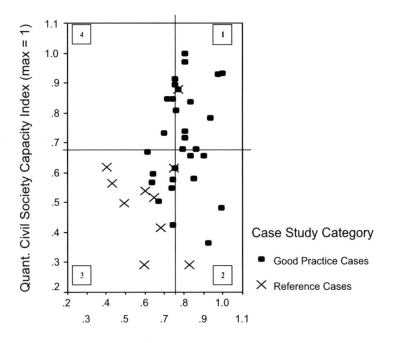

Quant. Local Government Capacity Index (max = 1)

Source: DISCUS aggregate database

Figure 6.5 *Local government and civil society capacity for sustainable development*

governing categories. These are also divided according to whether they were 'good practice for sustainable development' case studies or those in the 'reference' group.

The four quarters of the figure indicate the four different categories of governing, as shown in Box 6.1 (1 = *dynamic governing*; 2 = *active government*; 3 = *passive government*; and 4 = *voluntary governing*). To a large extent, the 'reference' case studies fall under the *passive government* category, while the majority of 'good practice cases' fall into the *dynamic governing* category.

DYNAMIC INSTITUTIONAL CAPACITY AND SUSTAINABLE DEVELOPMENT POLICY ACHIEVEMENT: A MODEL

It is clear from this research that local government is the primary 'mover' for local-level policies towards sustainable development. Our material indicates that in order to achieve policy outcomes, we must always expect an active government, which will lead the way towards active cooperation with an active civil society – creating possibilities for civil society organizations and citizens

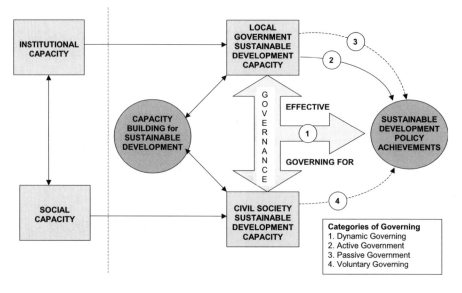

Source: DISCUS aggregate database

Figure 6.6 *Dynamic institutional capacity and sustainable development policy achievement*

to participate in the policy process. Active capacity-building measures will, in addition, enhance their opportunities for participating in the policy process. This activity does not replace the normal representative democratic process; it seems, instead, to add an 'intensity' dimension to the system of representative government. The four categories of governing are again presented in Figure 6.6 – the DISCUS model. Figure 6.6 illustrates how the various elements of governance and government interact to produce our four 'ideal types' of governing. The figure seeks to demonstrate that effective (or, to use our term, *dynamic*) governing for sustainability is most likely to occur when governments work closely with civil society agents in a process of governing, whether this is stimulated by Local Agenda 21 (LA21) or some other process. Moreover, 'success' is also directly related to the inventiveness, leadership, knowledge and skills of local government politicians and officers. High levels of institutional capacity relate directly to sustainability policy 'success'. The empirical evidence accumulated during the research programme therefore clearly supports our original proposition that 'there are causal links between [good] governance and sustainable development policy success'.

CONCLUSIONS

This section draws together the key themes that have emerged from the research project.

Local government autonomy

The research findings suggest that where there is evidence of strong governance processes for sustainability, and where there is also evidence of policy achievement in this field, then those local governments tend to have a high level of fiscal, legal and political autonomy. This is particularly evident in the Northern European countries. However, this is not simply a case of equating autonomy with achievement. What appears to be happening is that when local governments are granted higher levels of autonomy and independence, they respond to this by being more proactive and adventurous in their policy-making and implementation. Self-confidence, conviction and self-awareness seem to increase in line with levels of autonomy.

This relationship can be usefully characterized by reference to the 'tiers and spheres' dichotomy. When the various levels of government are perceived as being in a hierarchical relationship of 'tiers', each is superior to the one below. In contrast, 'spheres' implies high levels of autonomy for each level, with each operating within its own sphere of authority and action, in cooperation with other 'spheres'. This approach emphasizes the principle of subsidiarity, and although higher levels of government will always have some authority over lower levels, the principle emphasizes multilevel governance and cooperation, rather than vertical 'chains of command'.

The 'tier' model will tend to create a situation where local governments may have less confidence about their role, which, in turn, limits what they can achieve in terms of sustainability. There will be a tendency not to take chances or to be innovative in policy-making. The approach encourages short-term goals and a focus upon what is required by law. In contrast, the 'sphere' model tends to encourage local governments with a broader and more open approach to policy-making, a longer-term vision, ambition and a capacity to think 'outside the box'.

However, it is also important to recognize the role of central governments here. National legislation and policy priorities are key drivers in the sustainable development field, and although local governments may pursue innovative and adventurous policies in this field without central government support, it is clearly the case that such approaches will be easier when this support is present. Nevertheless, the DISCUS research indicates that the intensity of achievement at local level is, in large part, related to the level of autonomy granted to local government.

The role of the individual

A second crucial factor in local government sustainable development 'success' relates to the role of key individuals who drive the process forward. These individuals may be paid officials or politicians, and in the DISCUS case studies it was executive mayors who were most often referred to as 'entrepreneurial' figures with the charisma and commitment to motivate others and to promote the sustainability agenda. Officials were also recognized as being important policy drivers, often acting as the key link between local governments and civil society organizations and bringing expertise and new ideas to the process. However, in both these cases, there is always the possibility that the impetus for sustainable development innovation will be lost, or at least slowed, when a key individual leaves the organization. The process of mainstreaming a sustainability ethos within institutional cultures is quite slow, usually extending far beyond a normal electoral term of office, although there are examples amongst the case studies where this appears to be happening.

In several of the case studies it was suggested that both diversity in the ages of officials and the employment of younger officials benefited the sustainable development process. The implication is that such people might be more open to working in an innovative culture and that they could bring energy and new ideas and approaches from outside of the organization.

The influence that individuals can bring to bear upon an organization will depend upon the character, commitment and tenacity of the individual concerned, and upon the prevailing culture of the institution itself. If this culture is hostile to new developments, for whatever reason, individuals – however committed they might be – are unlikely to secure progress. Thus, although the role of charismatic policy drivers is important, such individuals are more likely to be effective if there is a degree of receptiveness within the institutional culture, or if the external climate – for instance, national government or European policy – is supportive.

Institutional capacity for sustainable development

We have used the term 'institutional capacity' to encapsulate the presence or otherwise of those capacities or capabilities – human, organizational, learning, knowledge, leadership – that can enable and promote governmental action in the pursuit of sustainability; as the previous chapters have demonstrated, when this occurs, there is a clear association between the intensity of sustainable development achievement and high levels of institutional capacity. This capacity does not come about by accident. It is, in the main, generated as a consequence of conscious decisions taken by local governments who have been effective in supporting and maintaining new ways of working and innovative ways of thinking.

Much of this process is about *institutional learning*, the process whereby organizations do not have to continually 'reinvent the wheel'. This ensures that, as personnel change, knowledge remains locked within the structure and practices of the institution and can be built upon as circumstances change. Actions can be taken to support and nurture this process of learning, and the DISCUS research clearly shows that those authorities who have invested in this process are the ones who have achieved sustainable development 'success'.

Key elements are investment in training for sustainability for both officers and politicians; the establishment of a 'horizontal' organizational structure that encourages cross-departmental working and a stable environment for sustainability policy-making; the adoption of sustainable development principles for internal practices, such as eco-procurement; and a preparedness to engage with civil society organizations as a central part of the policy process.

However, in addition to these organizational initiatives, successful local governments also have committed senior staff and politicians, who are prepared to prioritize long-term sustainable development goals and are linked to the political commitment and vision necessary to take often unpopular decisions.

This process of institutional learning is not an easy one to summarize or to practise; but it is of crucial importance for sustainable development because of the innovation that is required to address the complex challenges faced. However, as Nilsson and Persson (2003) have pointed out, this process of institutional learning may be best understood as a 'double-loop' process. The first 'loop' involves learning within existing frameworks, whereas the second 'loop' of learning actually changes those frameworks.

Stakeholder engagement and social capacity

Within the sustainability discourse the term 'stakeholder' has been used in a very general manner, referring to all agencies and individuals who might be deemed to have an interest in the sustainability process. In reality, the term could cover individual citizens acting in their own right; interest organizations, such as residents' associations or local pressure groups; and major actors (who could be legitimately described as stakeholders) who have some substantial interest in the locality or the issue being considered. Examples of this last group could include major landowners or local employers. The general point is that 'stakeholder engagement' can mean radically different things in each of these circumstances and that, in particular, the dialogue that local governments might have with organizations will be quite different from the dialogue that they might have with citizens as individuals.

Bearing this in mind, the DISCUS research has clearly shown that intensity of achievement in sustainable development is almost always linked to a high level of dialogue between local government and civil society. This dialogue is often referred to as 'partnership'. However, partnership is a political, consensual concept to be used to facilitate cooperation between agencies and individuals. A more realistic term would be 'alliances' – often quite informal in nature – between interest organizations and local government, within which local government is usually, and properly, the dominant partner. Nevertheless, the process of entering into these alliances for mutual benefit is an essential part of the sustainability policy process.

In so far as the DISCUS research was able to draw conclusions about social capacity in the 40 cities, it appears that in those cities that exhibit 'success', there are greater levels of civil society activity and knowledge regarding sustainability issues. Particular sectors that are supportive are local media (mainly newspapers); universities and the education sector; (in some cases) business and industry; and, unsurprisingly, environmental non-governmental organizations (NGOs). In general, where the intensity of achievement is high, there appears to be a greater 'buy-in' to, and civic engagement with, local government policy-making and action. In these cases, it seems that local government recognizes the contribution that civil society groups can make to the process; in turn, those groups respond by recognizing that they can have some influence. While this is not strictly corporatism, it does exhibit some of its characteristics.

It is more difficult to comment upon the level and nature of social capacity and civic engagement by individuals and the links to sustainable development achievement. However, it seems that where civil society has a tradition of being more active – for example, in terms of voluntary work, taking part in local decision-making and possibly voting – these cases are also the ones with the highest levels of sustainable development achievement.

Trust, consent and informal links

The DISCUS results indicate varying levels of what could be termed 'trust' by civil society in local government. This seems to be generally much higher in Northern European case studies than in the Eastern European towns and cities and in some Southern European countries, notably Italy. In the Northern European case studies, for example, there is more of a tradition of trust in, and recognition of the importance of, local government, and so there is a level of acceptance or consent to actions taken. In other countries, such as Italy, there appears to be a lower level of 'trust' and perhaps a 'grudging acceptance' of local government activity.

Notwithstanding the above, as a general principle, 'trust' tends to be between individuals rather than trust in an institution. Informal links between individuals develop over time and may form the groundwork for more formal and long-term relationships for sustainable development. Conversely, if these individuals move on, the partnerships may not survive. Moreover, there may be dangers in placing this 'trust' in a few individuals, rather than disseminating trust amongst the participating bodies.

We are unable to draw clear conclusions about the relationship between levels of 'trust' and sustainable development 'success'. However, the indications are that where trust in local government per se is stronger and more widespread, such local governments have a better chance of sustainable development success than where this trust is only related to a limited number of individuals in a local authority.

Local government as the driver of sustainable development

According to Agenda 21, local government is 'the level of governance closest to the people' and it is therefore best placed to pursue the sustainability goal of 'thinking globally, acting locally'. To a large extent, the DISCUS research substantiates this position. Local governments in Europe have been remarkably proactive in their pursuit of sustainability – in many cases, in the face of national government apathy or even opposition. Certainly, on the basis of the 40 towns and cities studied, it is possible to conclude that local government has been the principal motor for change, mobilizing local agencies and resources to secure objectives. Although other local actors have also been active, little can be achieved unless local government is supportive, and in most cases, it is from here that the initiative has come.

However, it is important to recognize that none of this occurs within a political or policy vacuum. Pressure for change may emanate from local organizations and pressure groups, from national or regional governments, or from the European Union (EU). Alternatively, it may simply result from a need to manage risk. In addition, as noted above, charismatic individuals may be appointed or elected and through the force of their personality may engender change.

The main point is that those local governments who show the widest range and greatest intensity of achievement are also those who have recognized their central role in promoting and taking action on sustainable development issues. These local governments are setting the agenda and acting proactively in establishing and maintaining partnerships and alliances both within the local authority itself and with external organizations.

To some extent, local government may be able to achieve change on its own. However, those cases where there are high levels of achievement are also those where some level of social capacity and a relationship between local government and civil society organizations exist. Thus, in most cases sustainable development achievement requires local government to involve external organizations in partnerships, both formal and informal.

The importance of incremental and pragmatic action

In those cities where policy achievement has been greatest there is evidence of a long-term vision and strategy for sustainability. However, there is also a recognition that in order to make change acceptable (both within local government and within the wider civil society) and for change to be sustained over the long term, progress has to be incremental. Pushing the boundaries towards more sustainable ways of living is a radical agenda, and actions taken too quickly or without sufficient dialogue may prove difficult to maintain.

The towns and cities in the DISCUS project that have been most successful have generally accepted this, recognizing that it is necessary to constantly support initiatives with information, publicity and explanation, linked to a continuous process of dialogue with civil society organizations. Small actions are both possible and acceptable and they lay the foundations for larger initiatives, while together comprising gradual change. This approach, which could be termed 'pragmatic incrementalism', appears to be the basis of successful local government approaches to sustainability.

The findings clearly show that environmental sustainability is the focus of all 40 towns and cities (with a few beginning to develop the social and economic aspects). The environmental dimension is the starting point for local government as this is where they have the power, knowledge and experience to most readily secure change. In many cases, this occurs through individual small-scale projects that can demonstrate good practice and can then be implemented more widely. Such projects may also be visible, so that citizens can see sustainability 'in action'. The wider global perspective is also being addressed through, for example, adoption of fair trade policies and climate change policies that raise issues of global responsibility.

Outward-looking local government

Given the high proportion of 'good practice' case studies in the DISCUS project, it is not surprising to find that most of them are active in city networks for sustainability and that they tend not to have deeply parochial attitudes. The towns and cities that are consistently high in achievement are those that have worked in European networks, such as the Climate Alliance, the International Council for Local Environmental Initiatives (ICLEI) and Eurocities, or more regional networks such as the Scandinavian Green Flag initiative. Involvement in such networks, the attendance of politicians and officers at national and international conferences and other events, and participation in initiatives such as the European Sustainable Cities and Towns Award open local governments up to good practice and experience elsewhere, which can, in turn, be interpreted and implemented locally.

A number of the case study cited have adopted high-profile marketing or 'badge' strategies – for example, becoming a 'fossil fuel-free city' or 'eco-city'. This indicates a level of self-confidence and it provides an opportunity for a city to showcase itself and its achievements. In addition to any marketing advantages that this might achieve (such as tourism or attracting employers), such strategies can also foster ongoing achievement because expectations have been built up and need to be maintained.

The inference here is that outward-looking local governments recognize that their responsibilities extend beyond their local areas, and that there are clear advantages to actively involving themselves in initiatives at national and European levels. However, there are some exceptions to this. Countries with strong centralized national governments may lead to a situation where local governments do not feel that it is to their advantage to participate in international initiatives.

Interaction with other levels of government

The relationship with regions – for example, the provinces in Italy and Spain – appears to be strong in many of the higher achieving case studies, and here there also tends to be strong links to the European level. However, the local–national relationship appears to be weak in many parts of Europe. Even in those countries where national government is actively supportive of sustainable development – for example, Italy and Sweden – the sustainable development links that local governments have are mainly with the regional and European levels and are less strong with national government.

While it is crucial for local governments to influence these framework conditions in order to successfully implement their sustainability strategies, local authorities' engagement with regional, national and European levels of government is also an opportunity for local government to influence future funding and support programmes for sustainable development effectively, and to get support for the introduction of sustainability principles within legislation and taxation.

Capacity-building for sustainable development

The review of capacity-building in Europe undertaken early in the DISCUS project revealed an enormous number of ongoing projects, many of which concerned international assistance (for example, through the World Bank); but only a handful of these could be categorized as dealing with sustainable development. Perhaps the most important vehicle for raising local capacity for sustainability both in local government and civil society has been the LA21 initiative, and this has a high profile in the majority of towns and cities studied. It is clear from the research that LA21 has been highly influential as a mechanism for disseminating information and nurturing understanding about sustainability and for building local policy skills.

However, although the concept of capacity-building has wide usage, there is less clarity as to what it might actually involve, and it often appears to operate by default rather than as a conscious, planned activity. In the case of the DISCUS case studies, the processes of engagement and dialogue appear to have acted as capacity-building activities in that they have prompted and encouraged understanding and enabled local governments and civil society groups to develop their skill and abilities in the policy process. While there is limited evidence of planned capacity-building, it appears that this informal process of involvement and dialogue has been both more prevalent and relatively effective.

All of this should be seen in the context of the Agenda 21 declaration that viewed capacity-building as the principal 'means of implementation' of the agreement. In reality, it seems that while some local governments have actively invested in building the capacity of their staff and politicians through training and educational programmes, there is little evidence that this has been widely replicated in civil society. This is probably a reflection of the potential costs involved and a level of uncertainty about how such programmes should be conducted and their precise objectives. Many local governments have invested in publicity and information programmes; but it appears that the most influential capacity-building initiative so far has been LA21 and similar processes through which participants have been able to learn about the sustainable development policy process while being involved in it.

From research to action...

This book has focused on assessing and evaluating the process of governing sustainable cities through an analysis of the DISCUS research. In Chapter 7, we turn to policy action and reflect on how this analysis can inform future policy implementation.

Chapter 7

An Agenda for Action

INTRODUCTION

The previous chapter outlined the key findings of the Developing Institutional and Social Capacities for Urban Sustainability (DISCUS) research and proposed a model for understanding the process of governing sustainable cities, involving both effective government and responsive and engaged governance. In this final chapter we use the research findings to draw together suggestions for action by local governments. Clearly, local governments cannot achieve sustainability alone. They will need to be supported by national and regional governments and the European Union (EU). But this book has focused upon the local level and local governments and so it is here that we direct our attention.

If there is any level of government that is most suited to act as an 'entrance door' in order to apply the findings of this research, and thus prepare civil society for the changes necessary to move to a sustainable development 'way of doing things', then it is local government. Local government may be the only government level that has direct contact with citizens, as it is often the 'local' with which citizens identify in benefiting from local services and in articulating their daily choices and preferences.

Developing capacity for sustainability within local government is the key to building capacity for sustainability within civil society. Local government in Europe will certainly need to undergo a process of innovation and even transformation if it is to govern sustainable cities in the future. The DISCUS research presented in this book allows us to highlight some necessary elements of initiating and managing this challenging process.

LOCAL GOVERNMENT AS A LEARNING ORGANIZATION

At a time when more and more public services are contracted to providers outside of the local authority, local officials as well as politicians predominantly need to know what social, environmental and economic implications different services have in order to set sustainability standards and conditions for delivery. Building up this expert knowledge within local government requires a readiness of staff for life-long learning, rather than trying to solve future problems with yesterday's education. In the short term, hiring expert consultants may help initiate this learning process and prepare the ground for a solid local sustainable development process. In the longer term, however, local governments must further develop their portfolio of expertise in order to be able to take part in the dialogue with local interest organizations and to facilitate mediation between them. Therefore, mechanisms that systematically help to identify the need for, and ensure the delivery of, training to both elected decision-makers and officers must be established within local government.

LINKS BETWEEN DEPARTMENTS

The tradition of local administration through individual departments and offices has certainly been useful in responding to the manifold and very specific problems of local society, allowing room for expert knowledge rather than just the knowledge of administration. The notion of sustainability, however, has highlighted the complexity of modern decision-making in local government. It is widely accepted that in a complex world, problems are rarely simple; thus, various forms of expertise built up over time in many parts of local government must work hand in hand, refer to each other and create holistic solutions. This requires a 'horizontal' approach – meaning that local government officers, as well as politicians, look at issues from different perspectives rather than delegating them to one specific sector – where there are adequate structures that facilitate everyday exchange and cooperation between various departments.

ALLIANCES WITH EXTERNAL AGENCIES

Although local government is clearly a principal decision-maker, it faces the fact that many decisions that affect the sustainability of the city or town are also made outside of public administrations and elected local authorities. Changing patterns of mobility choices, food consumption, tourism, housing preferences and other issues cannot be addressed by political decisions alone, but need to involve citizens in order to implement the changes required. At the same time, local businesses, institutions such as universities or churches, or community-based organizations represent a valuable source of knowledge and additional resources. Utilizing these in order to implement sustainable development policies requires an attitude within local government of welcoming alliances with external agencies and interests. Rather than fearing a loss of decision-making power, local authorities need to be aware that alliances provide access to different groups within civil society, whose acceptance of, and contribution to, decision-making processes is of central importance to a successful local sustainability strategy. Furthermore, these alliances may be a good starting point for developing mutual capacity and stronger relations of 'trust' between local government and civil society.

CREATIVE POLICY-MAKING

Local sustainability depends upon innovation. New and unusual solutions need room to develop. There must be a climate of self-confidence within local government so that new ideas are not perceived as a threat to the usual 'way of doing things' but are perceived as welcome and exciting alternatives, even if there may be difficulties in implementing these. Innovative policy-making for local sustainability could be described as the 'art' of finding and liaising with the most creative people both within local government and outside, and of encouraging and supporting them in developing surprising, and formerly untried, responses to local needs. Pilot or model projects, for example, provide a comparatively risk-free framework where single cases can be observed and assessed first, instead of taking general decisions at once. The positive results of such projects can then be mainstreamed into the 'way of doing things' and thus lead the city or town to a higher level of sustainability.

FACILITATION AND LEADERSHIP

Public participation should not be misunderstood as a mechanism for local government to delegate the responsibility for sustainable development to citizens, even though it clearly requires their involvement. Local government must be the driver that brings sustainability onto the local agenda, facilitates dialogue and manages planning processes. While input from civil society is needed, only local government has the legitimate authority to incorporate the conclusions from participatory processes within new policies. In order to build up credibility, local government must go further in proactively applying sustainability principles in its own management and activities, such as procurement and commissioning, energy and transport. Only then can other actors become convinced of the need to implement such principles themselves.

COMMUNICATION WITH CIVIL SOCIETY

Even the most sustainable local initiative is worth little if it is not communicated properly to all citizens and interest organizations. While in a knowledge-based society communication is one of the most important means of making issues 'fashionable', sustainable development competes with many other issues that are marketed and communicated aggressively. Local government has to respond to this by reaching out and being reachable. 'Reaching out' means using all available channels to communicate about sustainability issues and activities to citizens and interest organizations; this is achieved by being visible at community events, continuously cooperating with the media, establishing information services, or training staff in information and communication skills. Importantly, this is more than just offering information but includes the responsibility for making sure a message really reaches its intended audience. In terms of being reachable, this means that local government must be approachable in order to be regarded as a trustworthy and serious partner by citizens. In practice, this will imply offering citizen-friendly opening times and facilities, being able to answer requests and enquiries efficiently, and having systems in place for dealing with complaints and comments.

ENVIRONMENTAL AWARENESS AS A CATALYST

Although it is widely documented that sustainable development is not simply a new word for environmental protection, there is, as yet, little evidence that better economic awareness or social awareness serve as a starting point for a deep understanding of sustainable development. On the contrary, research confirms that a higher level of environmental awareness is clearly an effective vehicle to win people's interest in sustainable development issues. While this should by no means suggest that sustainability should be restricted to its environmental dimension, it underlines the importance of environmental awareness and knowledge of environmental matters with regard to local development, as it is often the environmental aspect that is most neglected. Within local government, establishing environmental management systems can be an appropriate starting point for developing an integrated management system for local sustainability.

VISION AND STRENGTH

The long-term vision for local sustainability may, in many cases, be very clear, easy to understand and even attractive. However, the path to sustainability often consists of numerous small steps and daily decisions that may appear far removed from the 'big picture'. It is therefore of utmost importance that local government – both politicians and officers – have internalized the vision and are aware of the long-term objectives of local development whenever decisions are taken, even if they may appear to have no relevance to sustainability. Finding the courage to stand behind an ambitious but distant vision, while at the same time implementing it step by step, is crucial for achieving results. Patience and sensitivity are needed in order to ensure that local sustainable development steps go as far as possible; equally, it is important to respect the maximum change that citizens will accept at one time.

NETWORKING BETWEEN LOCAL AUTHORITIES

Networking with other towns and cities both within and across countries creates a spirit of cooperation that can help to buoy up local authorities engaged in implementing sustainable development – a process that may sometimes be slow and characterized by challenges rather than successes. Meeting with other like-minded local government representatives and learning from them reinvigorates local action for sustainability 'at home'. Using national and international conferences as stages to present the experiences and good practices of a local authority builds up a positive image of a municipality externally, and a demand for the continuation of sustainability policies even if political will and commitment are not constant. In this case, networking with other local authorities can offer leading local officials and politicians a forum to present themselves as sustainable development pioneers. This, in turn, creates a greater sense of identity and confidence and thus strengthens the local process.

MULTILEVEL GOVERNING

To a large extent, regional and national government define the framework conditions and possibilities for local action towards achieving sustainability. At the same time, they can actively influence acceptance and awareness of sustainable development issues – for example, through taxation and legislation. While it is crucial for local governments to influence these framework conditions in order to successfully implement their sustainability strategies, regional and national governments depend on the information and input received from the local level in order to design their funding and support programmes for sustainable development effectively, and to get support for the introduction of sustainability principles in legislation and taxation. Local governments must therefore have an interest in liaising with other levels of government in their promotion of sustainability. However, these sectors will usually only take into account the views of local governments who have a reputation as being advanced in sustainability policy-making.

These suggestions for action are by no means radical. They involve subtle changes of attitude and values, which will, over time, secure the changes that sustainability implies. Sustainability is not a 'thing'. It is a 'way of doing things', which will need to become the normal and natural way of arranging our affairs at the local level in Europe. The DISCUS research has shown that this is possible and that success in sustainability at the local level is an achievable goal.

Appendix A:
DISCUS Fieldwork Methodology

COOPERATING PROJECT PARTNERS

The Developing Institutional and Social Capacities for Urban Sustainability (DISCUS) consortium consists of six partners and two consultation partners from consultancies, universities and non-governmental organizations (NGOs) in different regions of Europe:

- International Council for Local Environmental Initiatives (ICLEI), Freiburg, Germany (project coordinator);
- Northumbria University, Newcastle, UK;
- Åbo Akademi University, Åbo/Turku, Finland;
- WWF European Policy Office, Brussels, Belgium, implemented by WWF-UK, Godalming, UK;
- Focus Lab srl, Modena, Italy;
- Universidade Nova de Lisboa, Lisbon, Portugal;
- Regional Environmental Centre (REC), Budapest, Hungary (consultation partner);
- European Sustainable Cities and Towns Campaign, Brussels, Belgium (consultation partner).

The consortium also appointed an Advisory Board and a Panel of Practitioners. The Advisory Board, consisting of three academics from Italy, Sweden and the UK, working in the field of urban sustainability, was asked to advise on the development of the methodological and theoretical framework in year one, and to contribute to the discussion of the research findings in year three. The Panel of Practitioners (consisting of five representatives of local authorities from different parts of Europe) was asked to contribute, in year one of the project, to the development and refinement of the questions for the fieldwork. Both of the groups were invited to participate in the two internet debates in years one and three of the project, and to attend/participate in the DISCUS final conference in Fano.

RESEARCH QUESTIONS

The research was framed around three principal questions:

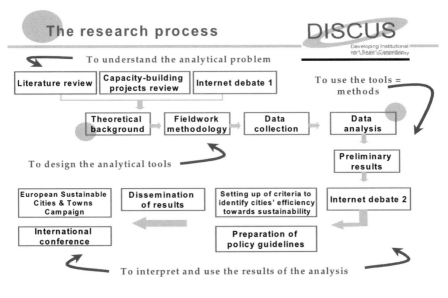

Figure A.1 *The research process*

1   What constitutes 'success' in urban sustainable development policy and practice?
2   What are the factors and conditions that permit or obstruct 'success' in local sustainable development policy and practice?
3   What constitutes 'good governance for urban sustainable development'?

In order to address these questions the research needed to examine three elements: sustainable development policy achievements; local government and civil society capacities; and interaction between local government and civil society organizations. Figure A.1 illustrates the stages of the research project.

YEAR ONE OF THE PROJECT

The first year of the project involved three related elements: the development of the literature review; the production of a report on capacity-building; and the development of the methodological framework. The capacity-building report was produced in order to inform the questions asked in the fieldwork phase on the nature of capacity-building for sustainable development. The report was produced after examining relevant websites and documents from across Europe relating to capacity-building, which revealed a huge diversity of projects and initiatives termed 'capacity-building', from a World Bank multimillion dollar-funded scheme in Eastern Europe, to small locally funded playgroups in the UK and Sweden. What became clear was that there was little evidence of any capacity-building projects specifically for sustainable development. The consortium also held an internet debate in year one, again to inform the fieldwork questions, and a number of academics, policy-makers and practitioners (including the advisory board and panel of practitioners) were invited to take part in this debate.

The research methodology required a combination of different methodological approaches to reflect the large-scale pan-European subject matter, with fieldwork conducted in 40 case study towns and cities. Document analysis, semi-structured interviews and a questionnaire with 'closed' questions provided the necessary triangulation of methods for the research.

The questionnaires were primarily used for quantitative data collection on the nature of the relationship between local government and civil society organizations in the arena of sustainability policy-making. In addition, they provided information regarding the different perceptions of policy achievement within and between local government and civil society organizations.

The interviews provided qualitative data on the capacities within civil society organizations and within local government in relation to sustainable development, and on the nature and impact of capacity-building for sustainable development. The interviews also provided material on the extent of, and intensity of progress with, sustainable development as perceived by the key 'actors' working in local government and civil society organizations.

The analysis of key policy documents was used to provide data on the strategies or policies that the local authorities had produced in the areas of sustainability planning and land-use planning (the main documents with which to judge whether sustainability was a core principle in policy-making).

Selection of cities

The towns and cities selected for the research represent all geographical areas of Europe, divided into four regions (these 'regions' are categorized for the purpose of covering the whole of Europe in the selection of cities, and also as a device for analysing the data). There are ten cities in each of the regions: Northern Europe, Eastern Europe, Western Europe and Southern Europe. The cases also represent a range of population sizes and 'types' of local authority structures or networks for sustainable development (for example, Barcelona Province and Modena Province, and South-west Finland Agenda.

The 40 towns and cities were composed of 30 'good practice' cases, which had already been identified as having an explicit and 'successful' sustainable development process in place, either from European Sustainable Cities and Towns Award winners, or from cases identified within the European Union (EU) Fifth Framework Project Local Authorities' Self-Assessment of Local Agenda 21 (LASALA). The other ten cases were a 'reference' group of those towns and cities understood at the time of selection not to have an explicit Local Agenda 21 (LA21) or sustainability process in place.

Table A.1 *The 40 case studies*

Northern Europe	Eastern Europe
1 Frederikshavn, Denmark	1 Tallinn City, Estonia
2 Albertslund, Denmark	2 Kuressaare, Estonia
3 Gotland, Sweden	3 Korolev, Russia
4 Falkenberg, Sweden	4 Anyksciai, Lithuania
5 Växjö, Sweden	5 Dunajska Luzna, Slovakia
6 Lahti, Finland	6 Gdansk, Poland
7 Stavanger, Norway	7 Veliko Turnovo, Bulgaria
8 South-west Finland Agenda, Finland	8 Orastie, Romania
9 Tampere, Finland	9 Baia Mare, Romania
10 Vantaa, Finland	10 Dubrovnik, Croatia

Western Europe	Southern Europe
1 Durham County Council, UK	1 Calvià, Spain
2 London Borough of Redbridge, UK	2 Granollers, Spain
3 Stirling, UK	3 Santa Perpetua de Mogoda, Spain
4 Dungannon and South Tyrone, Northern Ireland, UK	4 Barcelona Province, Spain
5 Ottignies-Louvain la Neuve, Belgium	5 Celle Ligure, Italy
6 Haarlem, The Netherlands	6 Modena Province, Italy
7 Munich, Germany	7 Fano, Italy
8 Hanover, Germany	8 Ferrara, Italy
9 Valenciennes, France	9 Thessaloniki, Greece
10 Dunkerque Urban Community, France	10 Beja, Portugal

YEAR TWO: CONDUCTING THE FIELDWORK IN THE 40 TOWNS AND CITIES

Thirteen fieldworkers were employed to conduct the fieldwork. The fieldworkers were already working in European organizations either within, or known by, the consortium: Åbo Akademi University, ICLEI, REC Bulgaria, REC Croatia, REC Romania, REC Slovakia, Environmental Centre for Administrative Technology, Lithuania (ECAT), Lithuania and the Estonian National Association of Local Authorities (the two latter organizations were funded via the Union of Baltic Cities, or UBC). The UBC and the REC offices took responsibility for identifying and employing the fieldworkers in the Eastern and Northern European countries.

The fieldworkers spoke the various languages that were required for the research in the 40 towns and cities and they had, or were required to develop, a broad understanding of the political and socio-economic context of the cities that they were visiting.

Training/briefing event

This part of the DISCUS project was perceived by the consortium to be particularly ambitious and challenging: it was in this phase that the fieldwork was handed over to the fieldworkers and they were expected to have a high understanding of what was expected from them.

The fieldworkers were therefore required to attend a training session, organized by the project partners and held over three days (at the end of year one). This event was the one opportunity for the project partners to meet with all of the fieldworkers and to explain the theoretical context to the project, the methodology and how to conduct the fieldwork. The fieldworkers were given clear guidance and templates to assist them in collecting the data and in structuring the responses. In particular, they were provided with detailed advice on the research techniques to be used: interviews, questionnaires and document analysis, as well as inputting data from the questionnaires onto a specially designed database. The training event was also an opportunity for the project partners to listen to any potential concerns or difficulties that the fieldworkers felt could arise, and to develop an effective relationship between the partners and the fieldworkers for the forthcoming year of research in the towns and cities.

At this event, the fieldworkers were introduced to the fieldwork coordinator, who was their main point of contact during their research, and whose role was to support the fieldworkers during the year and to assist with any problems. The fieldworkers were required to inform the coordinator of their timetable for the fieldwork, and the coordinator then devised a schedule of the fieldwork dates and locations in order to monitor progress.

The fieldwork year

The fieldworkers spent one month on each case study town/city to conduct the research. This month consisted of approximately one week preparing for the research (involving contacting relevant people for interviews and identifying relevant documents); two weeks in the city (conducting the fieldwork and transcribing the interviews); and one week inputting the data from the questionnaires and completing transcriptions from the interviews. To start the fieldwork process, the fieldworkers contacted the 'keyholder' in the local authority. This person had already been in contact with the DISCUS project partners during the stage of recruiting the city to take part in the project. The fieldworkers met their 'keyholders' at an early stage to discuss the research aims and objectives, and to explain in detail what was required of them in terms of identifying relevant people for the interviews and questionnaires in both civil society and the local authority. It was vital for the fieldworker to develop a good relationship with the keyholder and to make the research process transparent so that the keyholders felt they were fully briefed on the project aims and anticipated outcomes.

There were six to eight interviews conducted in each town or city, split between local government and civil society organizations. Fieldworkers were guided in the selection of interviews in two ways: first, by the project partners, who had suggested the selection of individuals (officers and politicians) in four categories:

1   a leading politician (representing the majority party – for example, the
    mayor);
2   an opposition politician to gauge the opinions of a politician in a different
    role;
3   a senior officer dealing with strategic issues – for example, the chief executive
    or city manager;
4   a senior manager with responsibility for sustainable development policy.

Fieldworkers were then guided by the 'keyholder' in the selection of interviewees,
as the keyholder was expected to have knowledge of the relevant persons to
interview in their local authority and in the civil society organizations.

For the interviews with civil society organizations, fieldworkers were
requested to focus on individuals whom they or the keyholder considered to be
engaged in the sustainable development policy process in the local authority. The
selection of four interviewees from civil society clearly had to reflect the local
context in each city, and the fieldworkers therefore had the flexibility to choose
from the following groups (and to cover at least two of these categories):

* groups/organizations who are 'active' in the local community – for example,
  young people's organizations, ethnic minority groups, women's groups,
  religious/faith groups and parents' associations;
* local business, environmental or social NGOs;
* semi-official or formal organizations – for example, the local media,
  universities, police, health organizations and trade unions.

These categories were developed following consultation with the local authority
officers and politicians on the panel of practitioners.

In most cases the interviews were taped; however, in a minority of cases,
the interviewee preferred not to be taped, and the fieldworker was therefore
expected to take copious notes. The interviews were semi-structured, permitting
a more open discussion of the issues. The fieldworkers posed the same questions
to civil society and local government respondents, and had sub-questions to
use as prompts.

The interview responses were transcribed by the fieldworkers into English,
focusing only on the responses to the specific questions, rather than verbatim.
The fieldworkers were also asked to include quotes to illustrate particular points
or issues that they felt were important to the research questions.

The questionnaire was translated into the relevant language by the fieldworker, and 40 questionnaires were distributed to both local government
officers and politicians, and to representatives of civil society organizations.
Fieldworkers distributed 20 of the 40 questionnaires within each local authority
to officers and politicians with managerial responsibility/expertise in the area
of sustainable development. For civil society organizations, the fieldworker
decided who received the questionnaire, guided by the categories identified by
the research team for the interviewees and by the keyholder. As a precursor
to distributing the questionnaires, the fieldworkers contacted each person to
explain why they had been selected and the importance of their contribution

to the research. The fieldworkers then worked with the keyholder to distribute and collect the questionnaires. In some cases the fieldworkers made a decision to sit with the respondents while they filled in the questionnaire to ensure that they understood the questions. This also improved the response rate for the questionnaires.

In each town or city, the fieldworkers were required to access a maximum of five key documents (policy or strategic documents relating to sustainable development and, where appropriate, the financial plan or budget). Fieldworkers were not expected to read the documents fully due to time constraints; therefore, they were asked to focus on the executive summary, main objectives, targets, policies and projects.

After the fieldworkers had completed the research in a town/city, the interview transcripts, document analysis and fieldworker summary (containing their own perspectives on the city/town, as well as the fieldwork) were sent to the fieldwork coordinator. Fieldworkers also entered the data from questionnaires onto a statistical package for social scientists (SPSS) database and sent this directly to Åbo Akademi University in Finland for analysis of the statistical data.

The fieldworkers were expected to organize all aspects of the research, and this was often a complex and time-consuming activity. In some cases this involved a number of visits to the city in order to locate and read relevant documents for the document analysis, to conduct the interviews and to find questionnaire respondents (and persuade them of the importance of taking part in the research). The language and terminology regarding 'sustainable development' was also problematic in some cases, particularly in cities and countries where these terms are infrequently used or less known. Despite these logistical and language issues, very few problems were experienced during the fieldwork year, mainly due to the commitment and expertise of the fieldworkers.

Fieldwork de-briefing

At the end of the fieldwork year, the fieldwork de-briefing took place and all fieldworkers were required to attend. This was a three-day meeting, which provided an opportunity for the fieldworkers to feed back to the project partners the knowledge and information that they had gathered while visiting the cities. In order to present their findings, the fieldworkers were asked to review the three research questions. The project partners were not expecting definitive answers to these questions; however, the fieldworkers' experiences and impressions of the cities were invaluable in helping the project partners to understand and comment on these complex issues in the range of geographical, political and economic contexts presented by the 40 case studies. The fieldworkers gave a brief presentation on each city and also gave their personal perspective in relation to the questions, so that the research team had a 'flavour' or 'essence' of what was happening in each city, but which might not be reflected in the data. From this feedback, the project partners compiled a 'partner' report of the key issues in each city (progress, institutional and social capacity, and capacity-building) in order to assist in their analysis of the data.

YEAR THREE: ANALYSING THE FIELDWORK MATERIAL

As described above, there were three major sources of material for the DISCUS study: interviews, documents and questionnaire data. However, a fourth major source of data – the fieldworker summary report – was added in the analysis phase, as this provided a rich context for each case for the research team. Before describing the analysis phase in more detail, we present some contextual findings from the questionnaires in terms of the response rates and the type of respondents, primarily according to the four regions. The fieldworkers delivered the questionnaire to 40 individuals in each locality. The average rate of return was 67 per cent, but there was variety between regions. Of the 1075 respondents, 18 per cent are from Northern Europe, 25 per cent from Western Europe, 28 per cent from Southern Europe and 29 per cent from Eastern Europe.

According to the local reports provided by the fieldworkers, the low return rate in Northern Europe may depend upon unfamiliarity with the vocabulary surrounding the main theme (sustainable development) and therefore a lack of confidence about completing the questionnaire. However, this problem was found in many of the Eastern European cases, where the response rate was actually much higher. A possible explanation may therefore be that respondents in the Northern cases were less motivated to take part in a survey.

The concept of sustainable development was, as a rule, better known among local authorities than among representatives of civil society. Local government respondents dominate in all four regions, especially if representatives occupied in semi- governmental institutions such as schools, universities, the police force and hospitals are seen as bound to the local authority. Representatives of governing institutions more clearly dominate the material from Northern and Southern European cases, while NGO backgrounds are most frequent among Western European respondents.

The number of questionnaire returns varied between ten for Tampere and 40 questionnaires in Italian Fano. Exceptionally, Romanian Orastie is represented through 44 respondents. But each case presents a unique blend in respondent representation. The strong presence of, for example, local government respondents implies that one or more other categories are relatively under-represented. According to the methodology we have chosen, respondents are thought to represent the locally acknowledged expertise on processes of sustainable development, irrespective of social position.

Our data verify the soundness of the selection process since 85 per cent of all respondents say that during 2000–2003, they personally have been involved through some organization in joint projects to develop skills, knowledge and awareness about sustainable development processes. Control of the effect of the criteria by which the 40 cases were selected shows that approximately 90 per cent of the respondents from the 30 'good practice for sustainable development' cases had been involved in joint projects, while many respondents from the ten 'reference' cases had not.

Since each individual case study in the questionnaire material is represented by a unique composition of respondents with different positions in local society,

Box A.1 will clarify over-representation of respondents in different categories, compared to the average representation for all cases. Thirty-one of the 40 DISCUS cases appear in Box A.1. In Romanian Baia Mare, the local government and NGO representatives together make up 93 per cent of all respondents. In Finnish Lahti, governmental staff and community group representatives make up 80 per cent. In Northern Ireland's Dungannon and South Tyrone Borough Council, NGOs and community groups together make over half of the local respondents, as do NGOs and semi-authorities in Danish Albertslund.

Box A.1 shows relative over-representation of respondents from local government in a number of Northern and Eastern European cases. A majority of the Western European cases have a higher than average representation of NGOs, but these organizations are also present in some Northern and Eastern European cases. The Southern European material is partly dominated by local governmental representation, while there are very few NGOs represented. The material from the Eastern European cases is diverse and reveals various patterns. The selection of respondents in the 40 cases succeeded in finding individuals, which in their own local context were considered engaged in, and/or experts on, sustainable development. This impression is further strengthened by answers to a question about the personal experience of sustainability work among respondents representing a local organization. Eighty-five per cent affirmed that they had been engaged in developing skills, knowledge and awareness about sustainable development in their municipality.

Analysis of research data

Åbo Akademi and Northumbria University were responsible for analysing the research data. Northumbria University was responsible for the extensive analysis of the interview transcripts, fieldworker and partner reports, and document analysis for the 40 cities. The interviews were analysed separately in two stages using the dependent variable in the original hypothesis (sustainable development policy achievements) and the independent variables (factors and conditions for policy achievement).

For each of the 'regions', the ten cities in each region were then ranked according to whether the data showed them to have low, medium or high levels of institutional capacity, social capacity and capacity-building (the independent variables) and low, medium or high levels of achievements (the dependent variable). The top five cities for each group, both in terms of progress/achievement with sustainability policy implementation, and process (institutional and social capacity and evidence of capacity-building between the local authority and civil society) were then identified. The interview data also provided information on the range and intensity of topic areas being addressed by the 40 cities and towns.

Åbo Akademi was responsible for the quantitative analysis of the SPSS questionnaire database. This involved manipulating the database to provide the relevant cross-tabulations and sum indexes (such as those for progress, combining all the environmental questions and the same for economic and social outcomes), as well as a capacity-building index using the relevant questions.

Box A.1 *Over-representation of respondents in categories, compared to average representation in all 40 cases (percentage compared to total average)*

Category	Northern Europe	Southern Europe	Western Europe	Eastern Europe
Local authority Average = 50	Växjö, Sweden (72) Tallinn, Estonia (61) Lahti, Finland (60) Tampere, Finland (60)	Calvià, Spain (88) Thessaloniki, Greece (69)		Baia Mare, Romania (64)
Semi-authority Average = 11	South-west Finland Agenda (25) Albertslund, Denmark (21)			
NGO Average = 14	Albertslund, Denmark (33) Vantaa, Finland (28) Stavanger, Norway (26)		Dunkerque Urban Community, France (42) Dungannon and South Tyrone, UK (32) Ottignies-Louvain la Neuve, Belgium (31) Munich, Germany (29) Haarlem, The Netherlands (26) Valenciennes, France (24)	Baia Mare, Romania (29) Gdansk, Poland (25) Veliko Turnovo, Bulgaria (25)
Community group Average = 7			London Borough of Redbridge, UK (28) Dungannon and South Tyrone, UK (21) Granollers, Spain (18)	Dunajska Luzna, Slovakia (20) Kuressaare, Estonia (17)
Business Average = 10		Santa Perpetua de Mogoda, Spain (31)		Dubrovnik, Croatia (26) Orastie, Romania (23) Korolev, Russia (21)
Other Average = 8	Frederikshavn, Denmark (19)	Celle Ligure, Italy (25) Fano, Italy (20)		Anyksciai, Lithuania (20)

The two analyses of the qualitative and quantitative material were then brought together to provide a picture and 'story' of sustainable development processes and progress in each of the 40 cities.

The chapters in this book reflect the development of the theoretical context and the consideration of the research questions through analysis of the empirical data from the 40 towns and cities.

References

Andersen, M S (2002) 'Ecological modernization or subversion? The effect of Euro-peanization on Eastern Europe', *American Behavioral Scientist*, vol 45, no 9, pp1394–1416

Beck, U (1986) *Die Risikogesellschaft: Auf dem Weg in eine andere Moderne*, Frankfurt am Main, Suhrkamp

Bourdieu, P (1986) 'The forms of capital', in Richardson, J (ed) *Handbook of Theory and Research for the Sociology of Education*, Westport, Connecticut, Greenwood Press, pp241–258

Brown, P and Lauder, H (2000) 'Human capital, social capital and collective intelligence', in Baron, S, Field, J and Schuller, T (eds) *Social Capital: Critical Perspectives*, Oxford, Oxford University Press

Christie, I and Warburton, D (eds) (2001) *From Here to Sustainability: The Politics of the Real World*, London, Earthscan

City of Munich (2002) *The Munich Perspective: Summary of the 1998 Urban Development Strategy*, City of Munich

City of Munich (2003) *Council Goals for Sustainable Development in Munich*, City of Munich

City of Tampere (2003a) *The Sustainable Development Report of the City of Tampere, 2002*, City of Tampere

City of Tampere (2003b) *'The Environment's Number One Through Co-operation' The Environmental Strategy of the City of Tampere for the Years 2003–2012*, City of Tampere

Coleman, J S (1988) 'Social capital in the creation of human capital', *American Journal of Sociology*, vol 94, Issue Supplement: Organizations and Institutions: Sociological and Economic Approaches to the Analysis of Social Structure, pp95–120

Commission of the European Union (2001a) *European Governance: A White Paper*, Brussels, Commission of the European Union

Commission of the European Union (2001b) *European Governance: A White Paper, COM (2001) 428 Final*, Commission of the European Communities

Dryzek, J (1997) *The Politics of the Earth: Environmental Discourses*, Oxford, Oxford University Press

Dunajska Luzna Local Authority (2000a) *Dunajska Luzna Territorial Development Plan*, Dunajska Luzna, Hupro Ltd

Dunajska Luzna Local Authority (2000b) *Dunajska Luzna Sustainable Development Strategy*, Dunajska Luzna Local Authority

Dunajska Luzna Local Authority (2002) *Environmental Action Plan of Dunajska Luzna for 2003–2004*, Dunajska Luzna Local Authority

Dunkerque Urban Community Local Authority (2002a) *Dunkerque Urban Community Contract (Agglomeration Contract)*, Dunkerque Urban Community

Dunkerque Urban Community Local Authority (2002b) *Sustainable Development Actors' Guide*, Dunkerque Urban Community/Extra Muros Consultants

Easton, D (1965) *A Systems Analysis of Political Life*, New York, John Wiley and Sons

Etzioni, A (1993) *The Spirit of Community*, London, Fontana

Evans, B and Theobald, K (2001) *Local Authorities' Self Assessment of Local Agenda 21 (LASALA): Accelerating Local Sustainability – Evaluating European Local Agenda 21 Processes*, vol 1, Freiburg, ICLEI

Evans, B and Theobald, K (2003) 'LASALA: Evaluating Local Agenda 21 in Europe', *Journal of Environmental Planning and Management*, vol 46, no 5, pp781–794

Forrest, R and Kearns, A (2000) 'Social cohesion and multi-level urban governance', *Urban Studies*, vol 37, no 5–6, pp995–1017

Forrest, R and Kearns, A (2001) 'Social cohesion, social capital and the neighbourhood', *Urban Studies*, vol 38, no 12, pp2125–2143

Fukuyama, F (1995) *Trust: The Social Virtues and the Creation of Prosperity*, New York, The Free Press

Fukuyama, F (2001) 'Social capital, civil society and development', *Third World Quarterly*, vol 22, no 1, pp7–20

Gdansk City Administration (1998) *Gdansk Development Strategy to 2010*, Gdansk City Administration

Gibbs, D (2000) 'Ecological modernisation, regional economic development and regional development agencies', *Geoforum*, vol 31, pp9–19

Giddens, A (1991) *Modernity and Self Identity*, London, Polity Press

Global Development Research Center (2002) 'Urban governance of accessibility, accountability, transparency and efficiency...', Global Development Research Center website, www.gdrc.org

Goss, S (2001) *Making Local Governance Work*, Basingstoke, Palgrave

Gualini, E (2002) 'Institutional capacity building as an issue of collective action and institutionalisation: Some theoretical remarks', in Cars, G, Healey, P, Madanipour, A and de Magalhães, C (eds) *Urban Governance, Institutional Capacity and Social Milieux*, Aldershot, Ashgate, pp29–44

Hajer, M A (1996) 'Ecological modernisation as cultural politics', in Lash, S, Szerszynski, B and Wynne, B (eds) (1996) *Risk, Environment and Modernity: Towards a New Ecology (Theory, Culture and Society)*, London, Sage Publications, pp245–268

Healey, P (1998) 'Building institutional capacity through collaborative approaches to urban planning', *Environment and Planning,* vol 30, pp1531–1546

Healey, P, Cars, G, Madanipour, A and de Magalhães, C (2002) 'Transforming governance, institutionalist analysis and institutional capital', in Cars, G, Healey, P, Madanipour, A and de Magalhães, C (eds) *Urban Governance, Institutional Capacity and Social Milieux*, Aldershot, Ashgate, pp6–28

Hukkinen, J (1999) *Institutions of Environmental Management: Constructing Mental Models and Sustainability*, EUI, Environmental Policy Series, London, Routledge

ICLEI (International Council for Local Environmental Initiatives) (2002) *Second Local Agenda 21 Survey*, conducted with support from UN Secretariat for WSSD, and in collaboration with UN Development Programme Capacity 21, Freiburg, Germany, ICLEI

Jänicke, M (1995) 'Framework conditions for environmental policy success: An international comparison', in Carius, A, Höttler, L and Mercker, H (eds) (1995) *Environmental Management in Kenya, Tanzania, Uganda and Zimbabwe*, Berlin, Deutsche Stiftung für Internationale Entwicklung, pp23–44

Jänicke, M (1997) 'The political system's capacity for environmental policy', in Jänicke, M and Weidner, H (eds) (1997) *National Environmental Policies: A Comparative Study of Capacity Building*, Berlin, Springer-Verlag

Jänicke, M and Weidner, H (eds) (1995) *Successful Environmental Policy: A Critical Evaluation of 24 Cases*, Berlin, Edition Sigma

Joas, M (2001) *Reflexive Modernisation of the Environmental Administration in Finland: Essays of Institutional and Policy Change Within the Finnish National and Local Environmental Administration*, Åbo Akademi, Åbo Akademi University Press

Joas, M, Gronholm, B and Matar, T (2001) *Local Authorities' Self Assessment of Local Agenda 21 (LASALA): Identification of Good LA21 Processes*, Report of the LASALA Project Team on Good Practice Selection and Analysis, Freiburg, ICLEI

John, P (2001) *Local Governance in Europe*, London, Sage

Kettunen, A (1998) *Kunnat ja ympäristökonfliktit*, Suomen Kuntaliiton Acta-sarjan julkaisuja yhdessä Åbo Akademin kanssa 96/1998, Helsinki, Suomen Kuntaliitto

Kooiman, J (2003) *Governing as Governance,* London, Sage

Korolev City Administration (2000a) *The Concept of Korolev Sustainable Development: Strategy of the City Transition towards Sustainable Development*, Korolev, Korolev City Administration, Department of Ecology and Sustainable Development

Korolev City Administration (2000b) *Ensuring Environmental Safety in Korolev. Main Directions of Korolev's City Development in the Field of the Environment until 2006*, Korolev, Korolev City Administration

Korolev City Administration (2003) *Municipal Objective Programme for Saving Resources*, Korolev, Korolev City Administration

Kuressaare City Government (2000) *Kuressaare General Plan 2000–2010*, Kuressaare City Government

Kuressaare City Government (2001) *Kuressaare Health and Sustainable Development Strategy 2002–2010*, Kuressaare City Government

LA21 Operational Action Plan (2000) *Pianodi Azione Operativo Agenda 21*, Provincia de Modena, Assessorato Ambient

Lafferty, W (eds) (2001) *Sustainable Communities in Europe*, London, Earthscan

Lafferty, W and Eckerberg, K (eds) (1998) *From the Earth Summit to Local Agenda 21*, London, Earthscan

Lowndes, V and Wilson D (2001) 'Social capital and local governance: Exploring the institutional design variable', *Political Studies*, vol. 49, pp629–647

Lundåsen, S (2004) *En föreningsbaserad demokrati? Ideella föreningar och valdeltagande i Sveriges kommuner under 1990-talet*, Åbo Akademi, Åbo Akademi University Press

Lundqvist, L J (2001) 'Implementation from above? The ecology of Sweden's new environmental governance', *Governance*, vol 14, no 3, July, pp309–337

Madanipour, A (2002) 'Editorial introduction: Collective action and social milieux', in Cars, G, Healey, P, Madanipour, A and de Magalhães, C (eds) *Urban Governance, Institutional Capacity and Social Milieux*, Aldershot, Ashgate

Maloney, W, Smith, G and Stoker, G (2000) 'Social capital and urban governance: Adding a more contextualized "top-down" perspective', *Political Studies*, vol 48, no 4, pp802–820

Marsh, D and Rhodes, R A W (1992) 'Policy communities and issue networks: Beyond typology', in Marsh, D and Rhodes R A W (eds) *Policy Networks in British Government*, Oxford, Clarendon Press

Modena Provincial Health Plan (2002) *Piano Per la Salute*, Provincia di Modena

Modena LA21 Action Plan (1999) *Piano di Azione di Indirizzo Agenda 21*, Provincia di Modena, Assessorato Ambient

Municipality of Calvià (1994) *LA21 Action Plan*, Municipality of Calvià

Municipality of Haarlem (1999a) *Strategic Plan Haarlem 2000–2010*, Municipality of Haarlem

Municipality of Haarlem (1999b) *Development Programme Haarlem 2000–2004*, Municipality of Haarlem

Municipality of Haarlem (2003) *Environmental Policy Plan Haarlem 2003–2006*, Municipality of Haarlem

Municipality of Stavanger (1996) *Environmental Plan for the Municipality of Stavanger 1997–2009*, Municipality of Stavanger

Municipality of Stavanger (2001) *Climate and Energy Plan for Stavanger Municipality – From Petroleum Society to Hydrogen Society. Local Action from a Global Responsibility*, Municipality of Stavanger

Municipality of Växjö (1996) *Environmental Policy, the Municipality of Växjö and the Environment*, Municipality of Växjö

Municipality of Växjö (1999) *Sustainable Växjö – Local Agenda 21 Strategy*, Municipality of Växjö

Nilsson, M and Persson, A (2003) 'Framework for analysing environmental policy integration', *Environment Policy and Planning*, vol 5, no 4, pp333–359

OECD (Organisation for Economic Co-operation and Development) (2002a) *Improving Policy Coherence and Integration for Sustainable Development: A Checklist*, Paris, OECD

OECD (2002b) *Governance for Sustainable Development: Five OECD Case Studies*, Paris, OECD

Ostrom, E (1990) *Governing the Commons: The Evolution of Institutions for Collective Action*, Cambridge, Cambridge University Press

Ostrom, E (2000) 'Crowding out citizenship', *Scandinavian Political Studies*, vol 23, 1, pp3–13

Ottignies-Louvain la Neuve Local Authority (2001) *Local Authority Political Declaration 2001–2006*, Ottignies-Louvain la Neuve Local Authority

Ottignies-Louvain la Neuve Local Authority (2002) *Engagement Charter for a Sustainable Development: Acting Together for the Future of Ottignies-Louvain la Neuve*, Ottignies-Louvain la Neuve Local Authority

Pennington, M and Rydin Y (2000) 'Researching social capital in local environmental policy contexts', *Policy and Politics*, vol 28, no 2, pp33–49

Peter, J (2001) *Local Governance in Western Europe*, London, Thousand Oaks, and New Delhi, Sage

Pierre, J (2000) *Debating Governance: Authority, Steering and Democracy*, Oxford, Oxford University Press

Purdue, D (2001) 'Neighbourhood governance: Leadership, trust and social capital', *Urban Studies*, vol 38, no 12, pp2211–2224

Putnam, R D (1993) *Making Democracy Work: Civic Traditions in Modern Italy*, Princeton, New Jersey, Princeton University Press

Putnam, R D (1995) 'Bowling alone: America's declining social capital', *Journal of Democracy*, vol 6, no 1, pp65–78

Putnam, R D (2000) *Bowling Alone: The Collapse and Revival of American Community*, New York, Simon and Schuster

Rhodes, R A W (1996) 'The new governance: Governing without government', *Political Studies*, vol XLIV, pp652–667

Rothstein, B (2001) 'Social capital in the social democratic welfare state', *Politics and Society*, vol 29, no 2, June, pp207–241

Roy, K C and Tisdell, C A (1998) 'Good governance in sustainable development: The impact of institutions', *International Journal of Social Economics*, vol 25, no 6–8, pp1310–1325

Rydin, Y and Holman, N (2004) 'Re-evaluating the contribution to social capital in achieving sustainable development', *Local Environment*, vol 9, no 2, pp117–133

Rydin, Y and Pennington, M (2000) 'Public participation and local environmental planning: The collective action problem and the potential of social capital', *Local Environment*, vol 5, no 2, pp153–169

Second Local Agenda 21 Survey (2002) Background Paper No 15, Department of Economic and Social Affairs, UN

Selman, P (1996) *Local Sustainability Managing and Planning Ecologically Sound Places*, New York, St Martin's Press

Sibeon, R (2002) 'Governance in Europe: Concepts, themes and processes', in Istituto per Il Lavoro (eds) *Governance and Institutions: Open Economy versus Bounded Contexts*, Bologna, Istituto per Il Lavoro

Skidmore, D (2001) 'Civil society, social capital and economic development', in *Global Society*, vol 15, no 1, pp53–72

Skinner, S (1997) *Building Community Strengths: A Resource Book on Capacity Building*, London, CDF

Sonnenfeld, D A and Mol, A (2002) 'Globalization and the transformation of environmental governance: An introduction', *American Behavioral Scientist*, vol 45, no 9, May, pp1318–1339

Stocker, G (2002) 'The challenge of governance', in Istituto per Il Lavoro (eds) *Governance and Institutions: Open Economy versus Bounded Contexts*, Bologna, Istituto per Il Lavoro

Taylor M (2000) 'Communities in the lead: Power, organisational capacity and social capital', *Urban Studies*, vol 37, no 5–6, pp1019–1035

Uhrwing, M (2001) *Tillträde till maktens rum Om intresseorganisationer och miljö-politiskt beslutsfattande*, Göteborgs Universitet, Hedemora, Gidlunds förlag

UNCED (United Nations Conference on Environment and Development) (1992) *Agenda 21*, Report of the United Nations Conference on Environment and Development, Rio de Janeiro, 3–14 June 1992

UNDP (United Nations Development Programme) (1999) *Capacity 21 Annual Report: Local Action, National Impact*, New York, UNDP

UN-Habitat (2002) *Principles of Good Urban Governance*, UN-Habitat, United Nations Human Settlements Programme website, www.unhabitat.org

United Nations (1992) *Report of the United Nations Conference on Environment and Development*, vol 1, New York, United Nations

Van Deth, J W (2000) 'Interesting but irrelevant: Social capital and the saliency of politics in Western Europe', *European Journal of Political Research*, vol 37, pp115–147

Veliko Turnovo City Council (2000a) *Strategy for Development of Veliko Turnovo Municipality from 2000–2006*, Veliko Turnovo City Council

Veliko Turnovo City Council (2000b) *Strategy for Sustainable Development of Veliko Turnovo Region*, Veliko Turnovo City Council in cooperation with UNDP and National Centre for Regional Development

WCED (World Commission on Environment and Development) (1987) *Our Common Future* (Brundlandt Report), World Commission on Environment and Development, Oxford, Oxford University Press

Weidner, H (2002) 'Capacity building for ecological modernization. Lessons from cross-national research', *American Behavioral Scientist*, vol 45, no 9, pp1340–1368

Weidner, H and Jänicke, M (eds) (2002) *Capacity Building in National Environmental Policy: A Comparative Study of 17 Countries*, Berlin, Springer-Verlag

Williams, R (1973) *The Country and the City*, London, Chatto & Windus

Young, S C (2000) 'Introduction: The origins and evolving nature of ecological modernisation', in Young, S C (eds) *The Emergence of Ecological Modernisation: Integrating the Environment and the Economy?*, London, Routledge

Index